How Do YOU Spell Customer Service? CA$H

Stories to Inspire Excellence in Client Relations

MIKE McGRAW

Sage Creek Press

TRAVERSE CITY, MICHIGAN

Published by SAGE CREEK PRESS
121 E. Front Street, 4th Floor
Traverse City, Michigan 49684

Publisher's Cataloging-in-Publication Data
McGraw, Mike.
    How do you spell customer service? ca$h: stories to inspire
    excellence in client relations / Mike McGraw. – Traverse City,
    Mich.: Sage Creek Press, 1999.
       p.   cm.
    ISBN 1-890394-31-9
    1. Customer service. 2. Customer relations. 3. Customer
    loyalty. I. Title.
HF5415.5 .M34 1999   98-86664
658.8'12   dc—21   CIP

PROJECT COORDINATION BY JENKINS GROUP, INC.

03 02 01 00 ◆ 5 4 3 2 1

Printed in the United States of America

This book is dedicated to my parents, Betty and Foxy, who instilled in me what is right and wrong. To my wife, Renee, and children, Erin, Lauren, and Michael, who live with me, support, love and care for me. To my many employees, who challenged me to recount many of the stories for this book. Without their efforts, hard work, and exceptional service, this would not have happened.

CONTENTS

INTRODUCTION

About 15 years ago, I launched a company called Entertainment, Ltd. It is a service business in which we plan
and execute special events—mostly for corporate clients.
These events range from a small company picnic to huge con-
ventions with live entertainment and multi-media presentations, with budgets ranging from several hundred to several
hundred thousand dollars. Each client is important to us. And
each—regardless of their budget—receives the same level of
service from our employees.

To fully understand that concept, you must first understand the difference between "service" and "services." "Services" are what we provide—event planning, entertainment,
catering, multi-media presentations, and other related services.
"Service" is how we provide them. And that's the key to the
success of our business.

ANY COMPANY CAN PROVIDE GOOD SERVICE

My wife, Renee, and I travel often, meeting with clients and
providing on-site support for their events. During our travels,

I really began to notice and compare the quality of service provided by airlines, restaurants, hotels and other businesses. I came to realize that it was not so much "what" someone did for us, but "how" they did it that determined whether or not we had a positive experience with their business establishment.

There have been times when I have been horrified by the service we received—or rather, did not receive—when employees were insensitive, inattentive, or occasionally even rude. Yet, there have been just as many times when I have been absolutely delighted by a simple act of kindness or thoughtfulness that made our experience a pleasant and memorable one.

Most importantly, I realized that any establishment—regardless of it is size, cost of services, image or reputation—can provide either good or bad service. Providing good service is really a very simple concept, but one that is too often overlooked by companies that focus too tightly on procedures, technical training, and bottom-line management. And it is really ironic, because the quality of service has the potential to impact the bottom line more that any other factor. After all, it is good or bad service that determines whether they keep or lose their customers.

FOUR LEVELS OF SERVICE

In this book, I discuss four levels of service. The most basic is what I like to call "simple service." Simple service is just that—simple, straightforward, uncomplicated service. It is the basic level of service that every company must provide and that every customer expects to receive. It is the kind of service that, if you do not provide it, your business risks losing customers. Simple service will not set you apart from your competitors, and it will not permit you to charge higher prices, but it can help keep you in business.

Simple service does not require the skill of a brain surgeon, the research of a marketer, or the talent of an actor. It simply requires a good attitude—a genuine interest in your customers and a desire to do what is right. It is those basic concepts of honesty, sincerity, common sense, politeness, respect and efficiency. It is a pleasant voice on the telephone, the smile that greets you when you walk in a store, a "thank you" when you pay your bill, a "May I help you?" when you look lost or confused, or a sincere "How is your dinner tonight?" from the waiter. It is taking time to understand what your customers need and doing your best to meet those needs. It is paying attention to detail.

Chances are, your customers will not even notice when you are doing things right and providing simple service, although they will leave with a positive impression of your business. Unfortunately, it is when you fail to provide simple service that they not only take notice, but tell their friends. Only what they are saying probably will not do much for your reputation or sales. Yet simple service is the foundation for all customer service. It is the first step toward reaching higher customer service goals.

Just beyond simple service are practical service and professional service. These two types of customer service often require an added level of understanding or management support, but are still basic to the success of any business. They sometimes mean rethinking policies, procedures or routines that were originally designed to benefit your business, but that do not necessarily serve the customer. They allow for the bending of rules under special circumstances. They require managers and employees not just to be polite and helpful, but to recognize, acknowledge and address customer needs.

Practical service is doing what makes sense for the customer and not just for the business. Professional service applies more toward attitude. Both practical and professional service should be a given in any business, but often are not. By providing practical and professional service, companies can begin to develop a loyal customer base and will generally receive solid marks for service, as well as a few referrals.

Finally, there is exceptional service—that which goes beyond customer expectations, that sets you apart from your competitors, and that has the ability to really boost your bottom line. It is consistently providing simple, practical and professional service, then going one step further. It is devoting your business to meeting customer needs, not just selling products or services. It is performing with a "can do" attitude, day in and day out, throughout your organization—be it a one person shop or a huge corporation.

It is these same basic principals that we have used to build our business. In fifteen years, we have never spent a penny on newspaper, radio, magazine or television advertising. Instead, by meeting and exceeding customer expectations, we have built our company based entirely on repeat business and referrals. We hire employees with a "can do" attitude and give them enough freedom to do what it takes to make our clients happy. We inform our employees that "no" is not an option. It works for us. I believe it can work for you too.

This is not a step-by-step, how-to book. You will not find a lot of statistics or research data to wade through. Instead, I have provided everyday stories to illustrate why any company and its employees should always provide simple service, how they can recognize opportunities for improving practical and professional service, and how they can boost their bottom line by providing exceptional service.

SERVICE IS A TWO-WAY STREET

I also believe that service is a two way street. As business owners or employees, we must provide solid and consistent service. As customers, we should expect good service and let it be known if we are not satisfied. When we accept lower standards of customer service, those lower standards soon become the norm, rather than the exception. Unfortunately, Americans have almost come to expect the worst instead of the best in customer service. Only when attention is called to a problem is that problem resolved.

For this reason, I also discuss ways in which you, as a consumer, can voice your own concerns when things are not quite what you bargained for. By letting a company know that you are not satisfied, you give that business an opportunity to make things right, you get that frustration off your chest, and hopefully, you prevent a similar problem from occurring with the next customer.

By accepting this customer service challenge, everyone has the opportunity to come out a winner. But it may take a little practice, as there are correct ways and incorrect ways to make requests and file complaints. I will touch on a few of the things you can do to improve the level of customer service you receive from businesses.

A Philosophy of Living

When it comes right down to it, providing good service is really just a philosophy of living. It is wanting to do what is right, showing an interest in your customers, and working hard to meet their needs. It is an attitude that applies not only at work, but when providing volunteer services, running a household, and dealing with the people you encounter each and every day.

Whenever you do something good, something right, you feel a sense of satisfaction. You will discover a new level of confidence in your ability to serve others, solve problems, and meet life's challenges. You will quickly learn that it is not so much what you do, but how you do it that counts.

Part One

SIMPLE SERVICE

Simple service comes from the heart and from the head. It is honest, sincere, thoughtful, helpful and courteous. It is keeping your mind on your business and on your customer's needs.

A Clean Soda Can

There are few things in life that I enjoy any more than an afternoon on the golf course. In fact, one of my personal goals is to play the top 25 courses in America during my lifetime. Whenever time permits, I do my best to squeeze in a round. It gives me a chance to relax outdoors where I can get some fresh air.

One of the courses on my "must play" list is located in South Florida. It was an especially hot afternoon, but I was looking forward to this fabulous course. After nine holes, my golfing partners and I made the turn and stopped for refreshments.

The soda can handed to me was dirty, so I asked the girl behind the counter if she would mind wiping the lid off. She was cleaning the bar and proceeded to clean my soda can using the same cloth she was wiping the bar with. Not feeling much better about the sanity of the can, I asked if she would mind wiping the can again, this time with a clean cloth. It was obvious that I was inconveniencing her. She quickly ran her dirty cleaning rag under the faucet, then wiped the can again, giving me a less-than-friendly look in the process. Finally, I just asked for a cup of water and a napkin, and I cleaned the soda can myself.

If her thoughts had been on serving her customers, she probably would have noticed the can was dirty and cleaned it before giving it to me. And even if she had not, common sense should have dictated that the can should not be cleaned with a dirty cloth. To make matters worse, she was unpleasant, never offered an apology, and was hesitant to remedy the situation. The simple act of cleaning a soda can, handled poorly by a golf course employee, left me with a lasting impression of this afternoon.

Ironically, it took more effort on her part to be uncooperative. When I requested that the can be cleaned, she could have smiled, said "I'm sorry," then wiped the lid with a clean cloth. That would have been the end of her efforts, and I would have kindly thanked her and enjoyed the afternoon. The day would have been much better for both of us. You see, providing good service is sometimes as simple as cleaning the lid of a soda can.

Common sense is a key ingredient
of simple service. Take time to
think about what you do and say.
It is important!

THE PIANO BAR

I love music and enjoy listening to a good pianist. Not long ago, I stopped at a hotel bar for a drink after a hectic day of negotiating airports, rental car lines and city traffic. I found a comfortable chair near the piano and placed my drink order. I noticed the music. The pianist was quite good, so I requested that he play "Perfidia," which is one of my favorite Glen Miller tunes.

The pianist thought for a moment and said, "I'm afraid I'm not familiar with that song, but would it be all right if I played another Glen Miller tune for you?" I said that would be fine. We chatted for a few moments. He wanted to know more about the song I had requested and asked what I liked about that particular tune.

It was a simple thing. He could just as easily have said, "No, I do not know that song," and gone on with his own repertoire of tunes. Instead, he offered an alternate and asked if that would satisfy my request. He handled the situation positively and pleasantly.

I stayed awhile and listened to the music. Even though I did not hear the song that I had originally requested, I had a nice conversation with a talented musician and a relaxing evening. Because he made a sincere effort to accommodate me, I felt good and was more than happy to leave an appropriate tip.

You see, providing service is more than just answering a customer's questions. It is responding to their needs.

If you are unable to fulfill a customer's request, make a positive attempt to offer an alternative.

The Doctor's Office

We have all heard the phrase "time is money," but never has this saying been more true than today. We have moved from an agricultural economy to an industrial age, and are now advancing into a service-based information society. Much of what we pay for today is based on the "time" it takes to produce that item or to provide that service. Yet, it never seems that we have enough time to do the things we want and need to do. Our days are forever hectic. More often than not, both parents work while our children still require just as much attention as ever. We find ourselves being asked to serve on one committee after another. There simply are not enough hours in the day to get everything done.

Those who should understand the "time is money" concept best are the professionals who bill for their services on an hourly basis—such as doctors, lawyers, accountants and dentists. Some of these professionals will even bill you if you miss an appointment without giving them 24 hours notice. Yet, it is often these same professionals whose offices we sit in for hours at a time, long past a scheduled appointment. I understand that doctors, in particular, have occasional emergencies that might throw them off schedule. But if you ask me, those who consistently schedule your appointment for 10 a.m., but never see you until mid-afternoon, are not only demonstrating poor organizational and management skills, they are showing a real lack of respect for you and your time.

Showing respect for others—especially your customers, clients or patients—is a simple and honorable thing to do. Keep in mind the cost not only of your time, but theirs as well.

Remember the "Golden Rule" that we all learned in elementary school: "Do unto others as you would have them do unto you."

RILEY

If you ever get the chance to visit San Francisco, I hope you will take advantage of the opportunity. It is one of those cities that is every bit as beautiful as everyone says.

One of my most pleasant hotel experiences took place in San Francisco. As I recall, it was a nice hotel—beautifully appointed, with plenty of amenities. But the truth is, I do not remember the color of our room, the cost of our stay, what we ate for breakfast, or whether or not we took a swim in the pool. I do remember Riley.

We had tickets to see "Phantom of the Opera" and dinner reservations at a nearby restaurant. On our way out that evening, we asked the doorman for directions. He said we would be very pleased with our restaurant choice, gave us great directions, and said, "Tell them Riley sent you and you will get a good table."

Upon our arrival at the restaurant, we mentioned that Riley had sent us. The maitre d' smiled and seated us. Our dinner was delicious. The service at the restaurant was impeccable.

Five hours later, after dinner and the theater, we returned to the hotel. Riley saw us arriving from across the room, rushed to get the door and greeted us by name. "Mr. McGraw, how was your dinner tonight? Did they take care of you? Did you sit at a good table?" He seemed genuinely pleased when we said that our evening had been delightful. He had been smiling each time we had seen him, but now that smile grew even bigger.

Most doormen simply open doors. Riley went beyond that—providing us with directions, allowing us to use his name at the restaurant, and following up with us regarding our evening. He even remembered our names. Most importantly, he impressed us as being sincere in his actions—showing real interest in our satisfaction.

Your customers will notice and appreciate genuine interest.

Is Fast Enough?

In our fast paced society, all sorts of companies and inventions have arrived on the scene "to make our lives better." Consider the fax machine, overnight delivery services, the 10-minute oil change, one-hour photo services and, of course, fast food restaurants. While this can be good, and can certainly give us more time to run our other errands and pack more into a day, "fast" alone is not always better. It still has to be right.

All of us have ordered lunch at the drive-through window of a fast food restaurant, paid, driven off, and then three miles down the road discovered that we had the wrong bag of food or that our order was not as we had requested.

It is very frustrating when you are hungry, but discover that you have been given a fish sandwich with mayonnaise instead of a burger with catsup, or a diet soda instead of sweetened tea, or that your fries are missing. You suffer because someone did not take the time to double-check your order. It is a simple matter of detail, checking the contents of a bag against an order ticket, but in the rush of lunch hour, someone forgot.

Many efforts have been made to improve and correct many of the problems that plague the fast food and other fast service industries. Most of the improvements have focused on "the mechanics" of providing service. If these companies can begin to focus on the "personal aspects" of the business as well, they should find even greater success.

Fast service is no better than slow service when it is not right.

DINNER RESERVATIONS

When coordinating corporate events, we often keep very odd hours. We may work all night tearing down the stages after an event or wrap up a dinner dance in the wee hours of the morning. Sometimes, we are fortunate enough to be able to dine at the more popular restaurants. Other times, we find ourselves in 24-hour diners.

I recall one evening when we had wrapped up an especially demanding, but successful event. It was 2 a.m. We were past being tired; we were downright punchy. There were a dozen of us who decided to grab a bite at the nearest Waffle House. When we walked in, I noticed immediately that, with the exception of one waitress, the place was empty. In a joking manner, I explained that we did not have reservations, but asked if there was any way she might be able to find us a table.

She played along, asking me to wait one moment while she checked the reservation list and table availability. After a brief pause, she said she believed she had one table left that could accommodate us.

The rest of the evening proceeded this way, with all of us playing our role in the game. We were in a good mood and, despite the late hours, our waitress made the most of the opportunity—remaining cheerful and serving us all by herself. In fact, we had such a pleasant experience that I left her a very large tip—which from the look on her face pleased her greatly.

No, this wasn't a five star restaurant, but the service was excellent and the tip every bit deserved.

Good service
starts with good people.

Santa's Helper

One year, Santa delivered four beautiful bicycles to our family. Renee and I each received one, as did our two oldest children. Santa remembered everything, even a child's seat for our youngest son, so that the entire family could go on an outing together.

A few months later, two of the bikes needed minor repairs. One had a flat tire; the other had a slight problem with the chain. I assumed that they were problems that we had caused. I gave Santa a call and he told me where I should take the bikes for repairs. It was a small hardware store in a local shopping center.

The gentleman at the shop was very kind, much like Santa. A big fellow, at 6'5", he even looked a little bit like Santa. He smiled warmly and said he'd take care of the problem. A week later, he called to tell me the bikes had been repaired and that I could pick them up. I told him I would get by as soon as I possibly could, but that this was an especially busy time for me.

As it turns out, things were even busier than expected. Furthermore, since it was still quite cold and wet outside, our family was not overly anxious to go on those family rides. One thing led to another, and it took me considerably longer than I had planned to pick up the bikes. I was really becoming embarrassed. I called the shop every few weeks to let them know that I had not forgotten the bikes. It seemed that every time I would make arrangements to pick them up, something would happen. It was just one of those things I could never seem to get around to, no matter how hard I tried.

Several months later, I finally stopped by for the bikes. The same gentleman greeted me, was just as polite as could be, and rolled out our shiny bikes. I was expecting to pay not only for repairs, but for long term storage. Actually, I was thankful that the store had not confiscated our bikes the way a dry cleaner does unclaimed laundry. He just chuckled and said, "No charge." Maybe he was Santa Claus after all.

Santa's elves keep the spirit of good customer service year round.

WINGS

One evening when I answered the telephone, a gentleman on the line said, "Are you coming to pick up your wings?"

A bit dumbfounded, I said, "Excuse me?" He responded that he was from the local pizza parlor, that I had ordered chicken wings, and should come pick them up.

I was not aware that we were having wings for dinner, but I asked him to hold while I checked with my family. No one had ordered wings. When I explained this to the man on the phone, he responded that they had a hi-tech system for tracking orders and that someone had called for wings from our phone.

Again, I stated that no one from my household had placed the order and that there must be a problem with the system. He said, "No. It's infallible. I know someone from your house called us."

To this, I responded, "No. No one here placed the call. You called me. And are you now calling me a liar?"

By this time he said that he would have to put me in his computer as a "bad account," I was really beginning to get frustrated. So, I asked for his name and the name of his manager. When indicated that he was both the manager and owner, I asked who he was responsible to. He responded, "I answer to nobody."

I hung up the phone and looked up the number for the district office in Atlanta. When I called, I explained what had just happened. They apologized, said this way not their way of doing business, and agreed to take care of the situation immediately.

I assumed that this was the end of the story and thought no more about it until I returned one afternoon from a business trip. While we were gone, our 9-year-old daughter had called to order a pizza. Our children were staying with a babysitter and they had all decided to order out for dinner. They knew nothing about this earlier incident and had called the same pizza place.

When she ordered, the manager told her that he couldn't deliver the pizza to our house because it was a bad account. Well, my daughter did not know what that meant and couldn't understand what the problem was. The manager then proceeded to harass her about the bad account. Finally, my 9-year-old, acting much more mature than the store manager, simply said, "There are lots of pizza places. I'll just call somewhere else."

Realizing suddenly that he was losing business, the manager said, "Oh no, that's not necessary," but my daughter just hung up the phone.

When I heard about this incident, I called the district office, described what had happened and asked for the number of their corporate headquarters. Upon hearing the story, the district office did not apologize or offer to help. They simply gave me the requested phone number.

I called the headquarters and spoke with the president's

secretary. A few days later, someone in their customer service department gave me a call. And, eventually, the local manager called and apologized as well.

Of course, like my daughter said, there are other pizza places in town, and we now order ours from their competition.

Everybody answers to somebody. In the end, it is the customer that every business is accountable to. Without customers, there is no business.

WAKE UP CALL

Because I travel frequently on business, I spend a lot of time in hotels. And because business takes me to all parts of the country, I am never quite sure which time zone I am in. So each evening, like most travelers, I request a wake up call from the front desk, which helps ensure that I will not oversleep. No one wants to miss important client meetings or events.

Each morning, the phone rings. Everywhere I go, it is usually the same—a recorded message that is brief, direct and gets me out of bed. However, one morning it was different.

There was this pleasant voice on the other end of the line. She said, "It is a beautiful day, Mr. McGraw. The time is 6 a.m. and the temperature is 72 degrees. Today's forecast is for sunny skies. We hope you have a nice day. Is there anything we can do for you this morning?"

This wake up call was a pleasant surprise. It brought a smile to my face and was a great way to start the day.

A bright and cheerful attitude is contagious.

DETAILS, DETAILS

Whenever we coordinate a themed event, dinner, conference or other activity that uses tables, we design a unique centerpiece. Flowers are always lovely. However, when clients allow us, we like to try something different and unique.

One of my favorite supplies to work with is mylar confetti. It is colorful, shiny paper you accent the table with that looks great. Customers love it, because it is a low cost way to create a festive atmosphere with lots of color.

Once, we made a centerpiece accented with bubble gum. The client loved it and complemented us on its originality.

Another time, when we were producing a hi-tech stage show with indoor pyrotechnics, a computerized laser show and an elaborate sound and lighting set, we placed "light swords" at each person's seat. These were small flashlights with tubes resembling the light swords used in the "Star Wars" movie. They were inexpensive, but tied into our hi-tech theme and were a fun way to start the day. The CEO, who thought they were a cute idea, even used one as a pointer to begin his program. Our client still talks about the light swords and what fun their kids had with them at home. The pyrotechnics and lasers may have been impressive, but it was this simple, inexpensive item that proved most memorable.

When there are cakes to be decorated, we make sure that the stylist does something unique to tie into the party theme. We do lots of decorating with balloons and props too. They can add so much to the atmosphere of an event with very little added cost.

Often, we transport our clients on buses to events or from the airport. When we do this, we like to serve refreshments. This in itself is not uncommon, as many companies will place a cooler with soft drinks on board. However, we always assign a staff person (in addition to the bus driver) to go along on the trip. They wipe off the soda cans, hand them out and visit with the guests. They are not tour guides, but they answer all kinds of questions. In essence, they are just a friendly face to welcome guests on board and make them feel more comfortable.

None of these ideas are very expensive and they are not very fancy. In fact, most are quite simple and our staff has a great time coming up with them. They have learned through experience that it is the little things that often please our clients the most. It is so important to pay attention to the details, because we know they often make the most lasting impressions.

The little things often make the biggest impact.

A NEW COMPUTER

Sometimes you have to work harder to make a purchase than a company does to make a sale. It simply does not make sense. What really scares me is wondering what "after the sale" service might be like when you cannot even get assistance during the buying process.

One of the major computer manufacturers was running a nationwide advertising campaign about the time we needed a new computer for our business. They had a wonderful campaign, which focused on the great service that they provide. In fact, I loved the ad campaign so much that I called to tell them so, and to ask for their assistance in determining which model I should purchase.

The receptionist took my information and left me on hold, then transferred my call to another person, who asked me again for this same information. She could not assist me, but left me on hold for some time while transferring my call to yet another individual. You know how the story goes. I spent the morning being transferred, placed on hold, and providing information without finding anyone who could assist me.

Next, I tried calling the advertising agency that produced the ad. They could not help me either. Finally, I went all the way to the top, calling a senior executive of the computer company, who did provide some assistance.

This company was great on building expectations through advertising. Yet, their system for handling customer inquiries was either too cumbersome or non-existent. They had difficulty answering a few simple questions from a customer primed to spend several thousand dollars on their product.

It is a simple rule of
customer service:
deliver what you promise.

Knock, Knock

We were on a family vacation. It had been a very long day for my wife and me on the road with three children. We stopped for the evening at a wonderful hotel with large rooms and an indoor swimming pool.

The kids had a great time playing in the pool. We ate a late dinner and then stayed up until well after midnight. Exhausted, we did not place a wake up call, but decided to sleep late in the morning.

Around 7:15 a.m., there was a loud rap on the door. Someone yelled, "Housekeeping." Then they rapped again.

I yelled, "Go away." Over the next five minutes, you could hear this woman knocking and yelling at every door on the hall.

I don't usually lose my temper, but this morning I did. Having spent so much time in the hospitality industry, I knew this was a common trick for getting off early from work. When you wake everyone on the hall, they go ahead and get up and leave for the day—so you finish cleaning rooms early.

Wide awake from the rapping and yelling, I dressed and went to visit the manager. He immediately apologized. Since we had two rooms, he offered to charge us for only one room. I thanked him and started to walk away. However, I stopped, returned to the manager, and said "No. We paid for two rooms to sleep in. We were not permitted to get a good night's sleep. Why should I pay for something that I did not receive?"

Hesitantly, he said, "You are right. I will definitely look into this matter and you should not be charged at all."

It was not my goal to get a free night's stay. My preference was to get a good night's sleep after a long day and to pay the room charge. The actions taken by this housekeeper were unacceptable. The manager, although he hesitated, recognized this and assured me he would address the situation.

Recognize what your customers expect and provide it.

Part Two

PRACTICAL SERVICE

*Practical service means focusing on the customer,
not on the company. Operations and procedures
should not get in the way of meeting customer needs.*

WHO'S THE BOSS?

It was 9 a.m. on a Monday morning in Dalton, Georgia. I made what was supposed to be a quick dash into the local discount store to pick up several items. The store was still fairly empty, and there was only one other person standing in the checkout lane. She was holding a toy Easter bunny and a $50 bill.

When the clerk saw the bill, she said, "Honey, I need to get me some change." But before she had a chance to do that, the phone rang.

It was her supervisor, who wanted to know how many promotional signs were hanging above each cash register. Instead of telling her supervisor that she had customers, she stopped what she was doing and took inventory of the signs—not once, but twice. The supervisor evidently did not agree with her total, as a lengthy discussion ensued that eventually required a second clerk to get on the phone and confirm that the information regarding the signs was, in fact, correct.

Finally, more than five minutes later, the clerk hung up the phone, went looking for her change, and completed the first customer's transaction. The lack of service we received was obvious. Yet, not once did she acknowledge the delay or apologize for the inconvenience to either of us. It was clear who she thinks pays her salary. The customer with the $50 bill does not come to mind.

Remember that it is ultimately the customer who makes your paycheck possible. Pay attention to your customers; take care of their needs first.

The Sandwich

One day I was on a job site and left to get lunch for our crew. I stopped by a well known national sandwich shop for ten sandwiches. After placing orders for the staff, I requested a grilled chicken sandwich. However, instead of the usual square bread, I asked if I might get the chicken on a round bun. The employee informed me that the grilled chicken sandwich only came on square bread.

I am unfamiliar with their sandwich making policies, but she had the chicken, she had the bread I wanted and each sandwich was assembled individually at the time you ordered it. For some reason, she simply could not put them together.

I tried reasoning with her, explaining that all I wanted to change was the type of bread. Again, she told me she could not make the sandwich that way.

Next—thinking that perhaps the bread count might be off with the cash register receipts at the end of the day—I even offered to pay for two sandwiches: a grilled chicken sandwich on square bread and a roast beef sandwich on the round bun. Then she could swap the breads between the sandwiches, tossing out what I did not plan to eat. She said she could not do it that way either.

In disbelief and rather amused by the bread situation, I became more determined than ever to get my sandwich the way I wanted it.

There was no manager around. This clerk was the only person on duty. I had just placed what was probably one of her largest orders of the day. Since she was not busy with other customers, I explained slowly and clearly two more times that I would gladly pay for two sandwiches in order to get the grilled chicken sandwich on the bread that I wanted. After nearly 20 minutes of discussion, she finally called the manager at home. Following their conversation, she agreed to sell me the two sandwiches. Even though it cost double what it should, I could at least assemble my own grilled chicken sandwich on the bread I preferred.

This may be hard to believe, but it really happened. The employee was so blinded by company procedures that she could not even see the humor in the situation or make a small allowance to please a customer. Either the restaurant's rules were too stringent or their training was inadequate.

Many procedures should really be guidelines and employees should be given the freedom to make reasonable allowances to satisfy their customers. Profits depend upon customer satisfaction.

Empty Tables

It is the *little things* that often make the biggest difference in a business. For instance, have you ever walked into a nearly empty restaurant and been given a table in a dark corner or next to the kitchen when there were clean tables in quieter sections or with better views?

This has happened to me many times. One such time, I asked a waitress if I could move to another table. She explained that the other tables had already been cleaned and were set for the next morning's breakfast, even though the restaurant was still open for lunch. I did not understand. Perhaps she was afraid she might have to reset that table. But, she would have to reset *any* table that I used. It really did not make sense.

At another restaurant, I was placed in a very noisy section, but needed to have a quiet conversation with a client. When I asked if we might change sections, I was informed that they could not allow me to sit at another table because the customers would not be evenly divided among the servers—thus effecting their work loads and tips. It did not matter that there were other customers waiting to be seated that could fill the gaps. It must not have occurred to them that happy customers might leave better tips. It was just their procedure and they stuck to it.

Sometimes procedures get in the way. They are established to give some semblance of organization, and that's good, but they should not be inflexible and they should not exclude customers when being conceived.

When you establish basic procedures for your company, ask yourself whether those procedures will benefit the customer or just benefit your business.

Lost in Space

Just in case you have not noticed, this is the age of the mega-store—those enormous warehouse size spaces that carry everything from gym shorts and tennis shoes, to prescription drugs and jewelry, to garden plants and housewares, to pet supplies and groceries. Drive through any shopping district and you will see a wholesale club open for retail business, sporting goods stores the size of a football field, and a hardware warehouse that is twenty times the size of the traditional hometown hardware store.

I suppose that there is some level of convenience in being able to find everything under the sun in one place, but I have never really been able to find what I was looking for in some of these stores.

You have probably experienced this dilemma yourself. You wander up and down the isles… searching…searching. Are the watches next to the sporting goods or the clothing? Is the cat food in the grocery section or next to the parakeets? Are water chestnuts on the shelf with the vegetables or is there an Oriental food section, and if so, where might it be? You need motor oil. You expect the automotive section to be next to hardware, but instead it is between the garden hoses and picture frames.

The truth is, many (but certainly not all) of these stores have been designed this way intentionally. Someone discovered that the more time customers spend wandering around their store, the more items they will see, and therefore, the more they will buy. Some stores have even cut back on the number of clerks available to assist or direct customers for this very reason. After all, while customers are looking for the milk (which, by the way, is always in the far corner of any grocery store), they might also pick up some bagels, ice cream, chips and dip on impulse.

So, instead of saving money by shopping in these large discount stores, customers may actually spend more money and more time without even finding many of the items on their original shopping list. This gives new meaning to the saying, "Time is money."

❧

By organizing your store and hiring staff to serve customers instead of frustrate them, you will develop loyalty that can offset slightly higher prices.

❧

The Washing Machine

If you have ever purchased a major appliance, or perhaps a large sofa, you are probably aware of the problems that can arise when scheduling the delivery of your merchandise.

Our washing machine retired for good one night after an unusually heavy load of towels. Shopping for a new washer was easy. We found exactly the model we wanted at a reasonable price. The challenge was scheduling the delivery. With three kids, the laundry accumulates quickly. We needed our new washer delivered as soon as possible. And we didn't want to take too much time from work to wait for the delivery.

The clerk asked where we lived and when the best time would be for delivery. We suggested the following morning. She said that time looked good.

To our delight, two young men arrived with our washing machine right on time. They hooked up the new appliance and tested it, then hauled the old unit off for us. They were careful carrying units through our home and cleaned up after themselves. The process didn't take more than a few minutes, and they were very polite and professional.

Not all deliveries are handled this way, but they should be. I have also experienced late deliveries that kept me away from the office longer than expected and deliveries that resulted in a mess that needed to be cleaned up. My business goes to the company that can both sell me the merchandise I want and deliver it with as little inconvenience as possible. To me, this is value.

Remember, your customers may be just as busy as you. Keep your appointments or delivery schedules. Try your best not to waste their time. If you anticipate any delays, call your customers and let them know.

Setting a Bad Example

Our company utilizes tents from time to time. We were setting up a 20' x 40' tent one evening for a health fair. It was about 8:15 p.m., and putting up a tent in an asphalt parking lot usually takes about 50 minutes. However, one of our employees forgot to bring the jackhammer drill for driving the stakes into a hard surface. Without the drill, or at least a good sledgehammer, this project could take two hours or longer.

Since returning to the warehouse to pick up the jackhammer could take hours, I jumped in my car and rushed to a nearby building supply store which was open until 9:00 p.m. I arrived at 8:55 p.m., but the doors had already been locked. There were still people inside, so I knocked on the door and they let me in. The employees told me that they were closing, but were sympathetic when I explained my situation. As a courtesy, they called the manager to see if they could get permission to help me. He said, "No. The cash registers are already being closed out for the day and I am running the day's results on the computer."

I asked to speak with him directly, repeated my story and offered to pay cash—with exact change—for two sledge hammers, so that they could ring up the transaction the following day. Very firmly, he once again said, "No."

I understand that he was probably anxious to get home that evening. Perhaps it had been a rough day. Maybe he had plans. Yet, here was a manager who wasn't interested in making a sale or improving his bottom line…who could not recognize an opportunity to help a customer in need. After all, no one rushes to the store near closing time for sledgehammers unless they really need them. More importantly, he set a bad example for his employees. He made it clear to them that closing shop was more important that helping customers in need.

This building supply store now has a nearby competitor. If the manager's attitude prevails at the original store, they are in for a real blow to the bottom line.

Remember that customer service starts at the top. If managers do not show a commitment to customer service, their employees never will. Seize any opportunity to set a good example and show employees the importance of customer service.

Team Work

"Team work" always has been and always will be an important aspect of customer service, because most of the time, providing good service is more than an individual effort.

A good example is when you dine in a restaurant and the server was great, but the food was not. The cook is part of the team, and the food is the primary reason you went to the restaurant. When cooks do not do their job well, it impacts the pocketbooks of the servers, because it effects the tips they earn. However, because cooks are usually paid on an hourly basis, the quality of the food they cook is not reflected in their pay. Yet, to satisfy customers, the cook and the server must work together as a team.

Salespersons are often faced with a similar situation. For instance, when we purchased new carpet for our living room, the salesperson was very helpful—pricing different carpets and letting us take the samples home to compare with our wallpaper. But the carpet arrived two weeks late. As a result, we felt a strong level of dissatisfaction toward the company, even though the salesperson had been helpful. It was unlikely that we would purchase carpet from them again. Someone on their team had dropped the ball. It reflected on all the players and may have cost them future sales.

Of course, it could have worked the other way as well. I have been in situations in which a salesperson promised more than a company could deliver and in which a server provided poor service in a restaurant that served excellent food. In other words, it takes everyone working together to keep the customer satisfied.

Providing good customer service is both an individual and team effort. Everyone must work together to meet customer needs and expectations.

No Longer New

Several years ago, a local bank made a sales call to request my company's business. They knew about the needs of a small company, were interested in learning more about my business, and wanted to assist me in any way possible . In fact, they went out of their way to help me convert my existing business loans, checking account and savings account to their institution. When I needed a line of credit that year, they met with me and had the credit line set up in a matter of days. They were really great.

Three years later, we needed to renew our credit line. Our credit rating was strong and we had paid off our existing credit line ahead of schedule. Business was going great. We needed the funds for a short period of time to meet the requirements of a major contract that we had landed, and we needed the funds quickly.

Instead of taking just a couple of days, as it had to establish the credit line, it took weeks to renew it. They needed more information. They had changed their approval process. Their rules for obtaining a credit line had changed and they hadn't let us know about the changes. Whether these were changes dictated by the government or simply internal bank changes, we never knew.

This is similar to "bait and switch," which is a term more often used in advertising. The bank had offered great service in order to acquire my business, but changed the way they serviced my account once the business was secure. The credit line renewal was eventually approved, but the approval process took much longer than it should have and this bank was quickly losing its personal touch that had initially impressed me. Now I'm looking for a new bank.

Be consistent in how you treat your customers. You can always improve your services, but cutting back on them will result in lost business.

The Video Editor

One of my clients was having a four day sales meeting in West Palm Beach which included a series of high tech video productions. Some of the footage was to be shot on site and edited in time for the closing presentation. Other segments would be pulled from existing footage.

I hired a firm to assist with the production. We had several lengthy meetings to discuss all of the creative, technical and logistical aspects of the production. The firm agreed to send two editors to perform the on-site work in West Palm Beach. In the meantime, they requested that existing footage be pulled. I had this footage shipped to them by overnight delivery so that they could get started with this project, completing as much in advance as possible.

When I arrived in West Palm Beach and scheduled our initial meeting with the on-site editors, I was presented with two surprises. First, one of the editors that I had met with did not attend, but sent a substitute unfamiliar with our project. Second, despite receiving the existing footage, the video production firm had not completed the advanced work that we had discussed. They had decided that there would be time to handle everything on-site, but had neglected to share their thoughts with me.

The job got done. The client never knew the difference and was pleased with the results. However, the lack of preparation by the video production company increased the stress level on this job and made the assignment much more difficult. Further-more, the client had unexpected needs that arose during the meeting and, as is sometimes the case, there were minor technical problems that required our attention. This reduced the time we had to work on the final production.

In summary, we all worked longer hours than planned or necessary. I also felt as if our pre-planning and initial meetings had been a wasted effort. In short, I was disappointed.

Do not surprise your customers. Communicate any changes in plans. Follow through with what you say you are going to do.

Do It Yourself

We talked earlier about the mega-stores—those huge stores that claim to carry everything under the sun, usually at lower prices than their competitors. Well, there is a hardware store that fits into this category, but has taken the high road when it comes to customer convenience and customer service. They understand the importance of building a solid reputation.

This hardware store serves the "Do-It-Yourself" market. They understand that even though "do-it-yourself" customers enjoy tackling projects themselves, they still need information on how to do the job. Their strategy of providing service and information in addition to materials has worked. In fact, it has worked so well that they now have difficulty living up to their own standards.

One fall, following a hot, dry summer, I decided to install my own sprinkler system. I am pretty handy when it comes to basic plumbing tasks, but I needed some assistance evaluating the different sprinkler systems available. I dropped by this hardware store mid-afternoon on a weekday, picked up several odd items I needed, then headed for the sprinkler section. They had customer service representatives scattered throughout the store, but all of them were busy due to a large number of customers. I waited awhile, which was fine, and finally someone offered to help. Yet, as soon as I began asking my first question, the telephone rang. He was needed to spot someone on a ladder one aisle over. He looked at me and said,

"I will be right back." I patiently waited for his return, reading specifications and information on sprinkler boxes.

Twenty minutes later, I was tired of waiting and tired of reading. He had not returned and no one else offered to assist me. So I left the items I had planned to purchase in the aisle and walked out of the store without spending a penny. I would rather have hired someone to complete the job than wait any longer here.

This store provided good service on many other occasions. However, I have noticed a trend that they seem to get busier all the time without increasing their customer service staff. In reality, employees can only handle one customer at a time. If too many customers are left waiting or are never helped, this company's service positioning may backfire on them. In time, their customer base and profit margins will begin to erode.

When you build your reputation on service, your business is bound to grow. As you grow, make sure that your customer service standards remain consistent and that customer expectations are met.

The Renovator

Whenever the conversation turns to building or renovating a home, tales often turn to nightmares. Our experience was no exception. We were remodeling an older home, keeping most of the exterior intact, but significantly changing the interior. We took three bids on the job, checked references, and made our choice in contractors. He agreed to complete the job for a set price.

We should have known immediately that we were in trouble. The project was late getting started. Like most building contractors, our guy had a time schedule that only he understood. Once he did start, he progressed much slower than he had promised. He apparently had several other jobs underway at the same time that required his attention. Not only that, but we were disappointed in the quality of work.

One day, we had another building expert come by and check some of the work. He quickly pointed out that the new beams that had been installed were not large enough to support the roof. I contacted our building inspector, who confirmed this. When we approached our contractor, he became angry and disagreed with us. Needless to say, everything went downhill from this point.

The list of problems continued to grow. For instance, doors did not hang correctly and windows were installed incorrectly. Our plans called for adding an 11 x 14 foot room on one side of the house. The contractor poured a foundation for a 15 x 20 foot room instead, which led to significant cost overruns.

When the job was 80 percent complete, the contractor left town. We have never heard from him since. I cannot imagine how anyone could have ever given this contractor a positive recommendation, but they did. We eventually hired another contractor to correct the problems and complete the job. Obviously, this was also done at our expense.

When you agree to perform a service for an established price, you should do it for that—unless your client makes changes and approves a revised budget—even if it means you lose money. It is much better to lose money than to lose your reputation.

❧

Reputations take a lifetime to build, but can be destroyed overnight.

❧

LAS VEGAS HEAT

Our family took a vacation out west which included a brief stop in Las Vegas. Since the kids were with us, we stayed in one of the large hotels famous for its family entertainment facilities. After checking in and getting settled in our room, my wife, Renee, read all the emergency procedures in the hotel information package on the desk. As it turns out, it is a good thing that she read this information.

This was a new building. The hotel had only been open around two weeks. Yet, at 1:00 a.m., the fire alarm sounded. We grabbed the kids, asleep in their beds, headed into the hallway, and traipsed down the stairs—trying to assist others as we went. It was scary and chaotic. We did not know what the problem was or where the fire might be. We received no instructions on the house PA system as the information packet had detailed and we saw no one from the hotel on our floor, in the stairway or outside who could give us directions. In fact, it was business as usual in the casino.

We made our way out into the cold, stood in the street and waited for instructions. Since it was late at night, most guests were wearing their nightclothes. The only employees in sight were the valet attendants, who thought this was a funny scene and were laughing since they could not hear the fire alarm and did not know what was going on.

After a few minutes, I went back inside to speak with the hotel staff. At first, they said they were unaware of the alarm.

After checking, they finally admitted that the alarm had sounded, but that they could not locate a fire. Fire trucks arrived and the firemen searched the hotel, but we were never told what they found. Ambulances were called for several senior citizens who were suffering distress that resulted from fear and over excitement, but the rest of the guests were ignored. Finally, the staff announced that it must have been a false alarm and that we should return to our rooms.

Some of us refused to return to our rooms until we knew the cause of the alarm sounding. While sitting in the lobby waiting for an answer, the alarm sounded again. Guests poured into the halls, crowded down the stairs and went back out into the cold. No one brought out blankets to keep the guests warm. No one gave any instructions. This time, the fire department did not respond. The hotel staff was completely unprepared to deal with the situation. There simply was no action plan...no one who would take charge of the situation. Guests were furious.

We remained in the lobby until 4:00 a.m. At one point, an employee came and told us our children could not stay where we were seated because it was a bar area and that they were under the age of 18. They failed to realize that the bar was closed and the inconvenience we were experiencing. Eventually, all of the displaced guests were ushered into this same area. After many complaints had been made, two hotel clerks made alternate room arrangements for some of the guests at a sister property.

Because we could not get an explanation for the alarm or identify the location of the possible fire, we refused to return to our room with the children. A bellman went to the room with me. I finished packing our things, he helped me carry them to the lobby, and our family dressed in a public rest room before heading out to catch an early morning flight.

When we checked out that morning, the hotel staff never apologized for the inconvenience. They simply presented us with our bill and told us to come back again soon. We never received a follow-up letter from the hotel. It was as if their reputation were more important than their guests, so they failed to acknowledge that there had been a problem. But the truth is, by ignoring the problem, they have badly damaged their reputation—at least among several hundred guests who experienced a nightmare of a stay in their hotel and shared their story with friends.

It is frightening to think of what could have happened if this had been a real emergency. What would have happened if I had stayed out late in the casinos while the rest of my family slept? How would elderly persons have escaped without assistance? What if there really had been a fire in this hotel filled with thousands of guests and the fire department had not responded? A few employees had shown some compassion for our dilemma, but they were in the minority. The employees were not trained to handle an emergency.

A crisis situation calls for compassion and common sense. Your employees should be prepared to handle potential crisis situations.

Dinosaur Suits

A good dry cleaner is sometimes hard to find. There are those who consistently break buttons on your best shirts, which you never discover until you are in a hurry to dress for an important meeting. Some have questionable systems for tracking your clothing. And, of course, there is always the question of why it costs so much more to launder a woman's cotton blouse than a man's cotton dress shirt.

To make our search for a dry cleaner even more difficult, our cleaning needs are out of the ordinary. We did find a local dry cleaner, just five minutes away, who provides basic cleaning services and does an nice job with our suits, shirts and dresses, but he turns away the rest of our business. Since many of our items are unusual—patriotic bunting, American flags, table cloths, chicken outfits, super hero costumes and purple dinosaur suits—he made the business decision not to accept them.

However, we found a dry cleaner 20 minutes away that was very appreciative of our business. The owner laughed at our odd assortment of items and considered them a challenge. Even though our items required special handling, he accepted them with a smile. And because he is so pleasant to do business with, we don't mind driving the extra distance for his services.

In some industries, all you have to do is meet basic customer expectations in order to set yourself apart from the competition. Just imagine what you could do by excelling in customer service!

NICKELS AND DIMES

We recently handled a meeting at a fairly new convention center in Atlanta. As scheduled, we arrived a day early to set up for the meeting. It was summer, and we were experiencing one of our southern heat waves. It was well over 90 degrees and very humid, so we were alarmed to discover that we were not provided with air conditioning in the ballroom. When I checked, the convention center staff said they could turn the air conditioning on, but that it would cost extra.

We had several displays that needed to be hung outside the room. The conference center informed me that their staff must hang all signs and that there would be an additional charge for this service.

Upon my client's arrival from Denver, she requested permission to store nine boxes in their assigned meeting room. The conference center agreed, but informed her that there would be an additional charge. She elected to pile the boxes in her hotel room and transport them a second time the following day to the meeting room.

During the meeting finale, confetti cannons were used for a special effect. We had already agreed to pay an additional clean up fee for the confetti streamers. However, when the cleanup crew arrived, they informed us that there would be an extra fee for removing streamers from the chandelier. They did not consider cleaning the chandelier part of their original agreement.

In essence, the convention center not only charged a base fee for the meeting, they nickeled and dimed us to death once we arrived. We had already paid a considerable amount for this event, but were hit with many unexpected additional charges.

When establishing fees and billing procedures, think of your customers as well as your bank account. Consider building all services into a basic fee. Be sure to explain your billing procedures to your customers in advance if there is any possibility for confusion or misunderstanding.

Part Three

PROFESSIONAL SERVICE

Professional service is a matter of attitude. It is being able to evaluate a situation and respond appropriately.

The Maitre d'

One way of providing professional service is by providing a unique, personal touch. This is especially important in the service industry, but can be applied to almost any business.

A prime example of someone who provides that personal touch is the maitre d' who greeted us as we arrived one evening for dinner at the Arizona Biltmore. They run a five star restaurant, so we had great expectations before we were even seated. And this gentleman did not disappoint us. A maitre d' is trained to be courteous and gracious. He was this and more.

He stepped toward us in greeting, rather than waiting for us to arrive at his station. He seemed intuitive, knowing exactly the right way to address each member of our party. It was obvious watching him move through the restaurant that his etiquette was impeccable and that he could make anyone from a pauper to a prince feel welcome in his restaurant.

Not only was he gracious, he seated us individually and looked after us—stopping by the table often, but without being intrusive. He made sure that we were never without the water, drinks or other services we needed, that our food was prepared to our liking, and—most of all—that we were enjoying our evening.

I cannot recall what I ate that evening—although I know that it was excellent—but thanks to the maitre d', I will always remember our evening at the Arizona Biltmore as a first class dining experience.

❦

Mark your service by letting your personality and talents shine through. Show your customers that you enjoy what you do.

❦

THE VIRUS

When we purchased three new computers for our office, we also purchased the extended service agreements. Within two months, we encountered a host of technical problems that we could not identify or resolve on our own. Working closely with the technical support staffs for the various software programs we were able to determine that our problems were not software related, so we contacted the hardware service company for help.

They attempted to resolve our problems by telephone—to no avail. When we explained that our business had just about shut down because of the computer problems, they agreed to send someone out in two days.

The repairman was very pleasant and immediately identified the problem. He detected a rare computer "virus." Since the virus was not hardware related, he was not required to perform any repairs. He could have left immediately upon identifying the problem. However, he knew how much we needed our computers up and running, and he knew how to fix the problem. So we encouraged him to proceed. Within minutes, we were back in business.

Instead of saying, "It is not my job," or "I am not permitted to perform this type of repair," the repairman did what he could to meet our needs. He tried and succeeded. It was a simple act that we really noticed and appreciated. He left us with a good feeling about his company.

Going beyond your normal duties to
meet customer needs is a great way
to build customer loyalty.

THE LOST WEDDING RING

When I was younger, I was fortunate enough to work for the cabin service department at Delta Airlines, which was responsible for cleaning and restocking the cabins of all airplanes. We were also responsible for cleaning out the lavatories on the planes when they came in for refueling. I was one of the guys on those many little vehicles that circled the plane while passengers were boarding. I would pull up next to the plane, attach a long tube, and suction out the waste water. It may sound messy, but it was really a fairly simple process.

One day, I received a call on my walkie-talkie that a woman had lost her diamond wedding ring in the lavatory of the plane I was servicing. Without giving it much thought, I drove out to a remote runway that was not currently being used, dumped out the contents of the lavatory, sorted through it with a stick, then cleaned up the area. Unfortunately, I never found the ring and eventually had to get back and service the other planes.

A few weeks later, a senior vice president tracked me down and presented me with the Outstanding Customer Service Award, which is the highest award for customer service presented by Delta Airlines. The honest truth is, at the time, I had to ask him what it was for. He said that a woman had called to find out who had gone to the trouble to look for her wedding ring. Even though I had not found the ring, it meant a great deal to her that someone had taken the time to look for it.

Granted, it was the only time I ever had to sort through lavatory waste, but I just considered it part of doing my job. In fact, I was disappointed because I could not find the ring for the customer. But what I realized was that even though we are not always successful, it is really the effort to help the customer that leaves the lasting impression.

Providing service is not everything. It is the desire and willingness to provide service that counts the most.

Two Left Shoes

There is a department store, like most I suppose, where employees are taught to compliment customers on their fine choices as they are ringing up the sale. I guess it is meant to eliminate those last minute feelings of buyer's remorse.

Well, a friend of mine had just bought a pair of ladies heels at this department store, and the clerk had raved about the comfort and styling of these shoes, noting that she had a pair herself. Later, upstairs in the dress department, another clerk told my friend how professional she would look in her new striped suit as she folded and bagged the merchandise.

At home, 35 miles away, my friend discovered not only that she had purchased two left shoes in different sizes, but that her new suit still had one of those security devices attached that would spew ink on her clothes if she tried to remove it. An hour and a half later, she had made the round trip to pick up the right shoe and have the inking device removed.

A few months later, she purchased a sweater at this same department store and a different clerk complimented her on her fine eye for fashion. Recalling her previous experience, my friend reminded the clerk to be sure and remove the security tag. Believe it or not, when she got home and began dressing for a party, she noticed a familiar white plastic tag securely fixed to her sweater.

Once again, by getting so wrapped up in complimenting

her customer, a clerk had failed to perform a routine task. The compliments were nice, but the error was a real headache. That sweater was the last item my friend purchased at this department store. Her store credit card was promptly cut in half and returned with her final payment.

Although it is important to be friendly and nice to be complimentary, we also need to keep our minds on doing our jobs correctly.

Overdrawn and Outraged

I am the world's worst when it comes to balancing my checking account. Fortunately, my wife, Renee, is the best in-house accountant you could ask for, so I relinquish these duties to her.

One day, I received a notice from my bank stating that I had overdrawn my account. Since I had recently made a deposit to this account, I knew there must be a mistake. So, I called the bank to review the situation.

The customer service representative who handled my call was very frank and direct. Without asking me any questions, she said my account was overdrawn and that I should immediately make a deposit to cover the overdraft. I was offended by her manner and tone of voice, which clearly accused me of doing something wrong.

Turning to my favorite in-house accountant, we found the deposit slip from the previous week and took it by the bank. As it turns out, the bank had, in fact, made an error and failed to deposit the funds to my account.

Banks, like any other business, make occasional errors when handling thousands of transactions each day. This is understandable and acceptable, provided the errors are infrequent and quickly corrected. The attitude of the customer service representative, however, signifies a more difficult problem—not only one of failure to investigate the facts, but of attitude.

It pays to give the customer the benefit of the doubt and to research a problem. As with our legal system, in which we are innocent until proven guilty, customers should be right until proven wrong. Even then, the situation requires careful handling.

Never "accuse" a customer of anything. If there is a problem, check your facts and approach the customer in a courteous and thoughtful manner.

Delivered by a Stranger

As any mother can tell you, having a baby is a very personal thing. Selecting a doctor to deliver your baby is not a task taken lightly by most couples. After all, a woman will visit her doctor regularly for at least nine months, then spend some of her most emotional and private moments in their care.

Renee and I have three children. The doctor we had chosen had delivered our first two children. By the time Renee was expecting our third child, this doctor had taken on partners, and she was informed that, depending upon rotations, one of the partners might deliver our baby.

We were not pleased with this change in procedures. After all, Renee had only seen the other partners once during her pregnancy. They did not know her as well as her own doctor. When we originally selected our doctor, we were told that he would be there to deliver our babies.

We explained to our doctor that we had chosen him—not an associate of his—as our obstetrician. We wanted him to know that it was important to us that he deliver our child after caring for Renee for nine months. As it turns out, the new procedures were given priority over our concerns and request.

One of the new partners was on call when Renee went into labor, so a stranger delivered our child. Medically, everything went just fine. Emotionally, we were saddled with an extra burden. We needed to have a sense of security and comfort at this time. Instead, we felt our doctor had let us down.

Perhaps the change made by our obstetrician is common now. I know that any doctors who are "on call" must keep terrible schedules and like anyone else, need time away from work. However, I also know that this is a recent development, and that for years, doctors always delivered the babies of their patients except in very unusual circumstances. Why must we accept this change now?

If I hired a particular artist to do a painting, I would not expect another painter to provide the finished product. It is not only a matter of style, it is a matter of ethics.

We are still friends with this doctor and Renee is still one of his patients. We know he is a good doctor and a good person. We just regret that in this day and time, procedures are becoming more important than personal attention.

If you provide professional, personal or artistic services, keep in mind that your customers have chosen you for very personal reasons. If you are making changes in the way you provide your services, do not forget your customers' feelings and needs.

OVERCOMING ADVERSITY

It was one of those long weeks of unbearable days. We were all exhausted. The phone just would not stop ringing. It seemed like everything we were doing was a challenge. We needed a break. So I took the staff to a local restaurant for dinner and drinks.

I ordered a Bloody Mary. When it arrived, I noticed the celery was dirty. Obviously, it had not been washed before being placed in my drink. I pointed this out to the waitress, who removed the celery from my drink and walked away. We watched in silence as she did this, curious about what her next step might be. She returned a few moments later with a clean celery stalk, which she placed in my drink.

Calmly and patiently, I thanked her for the celery but pointed out that if the celery was dirty and had been placed in my drink, then my drink was also dirty.

At that moment, it was as if a light bulb had just been turned on in her head. She laughed, apologized and was back in a flash with a fresh drink and a smile. Not more than 20 seconds later, the manager also appeared at our table to ask how my Bloody Mary was. She apologized for the problem with the drink and asked us to let her know if we needed anything at all.

Throughout our meal, the waitress made jokes about the celery, kept the mood light and really took care of us. She turned a potentially negative situation into a positive one, thus going from the hot seat to the penthouse in our minds. Despite the long week and the dirty celery, our day ended on a positive note.

Never be afraid to turn the table on a negative situation. Apologize, move on and keep a positive attitude. After all, everyone makes mistakes from time to time.

Monsoon

Sometimes things just go wrong. There is nothing we can do to stop or change certain things from happening, but we can find positive ways to deal with challenging situations.

The weather had been beautiful, but the forecast called for rain. My client decided to take a chance and proceed with an outdoor employee picnic. An hour into the event, black clouds rolled in and the monsoon season began. The rain came down in torrents, children squealed, and our client looked to us for an answer. We could not stop the rain, thunder and lightening, but it was up to us to find a way to salvage this event.

For safety reasons, all 300 people were moved indoors to the employee cafeteria. Then we began the task of assessing what could be salvaged and which activities could be performed indoors. The face painters and caricaturists were easy to move inside. The remaining activities were a little more difficult.

There we were—drenched to the bones with wet t-shirts clinging to our bodies, stringy, wet hair, melting makeup and squeaky shoes—peddling our popcorn, cotton candy, snow cones and ice cream up and down the aisles of this cafeteria. We looked so ridiculous that we just played it up by smiling and having fun. Slowly, the crowd joined in and before long, people were having a good time despite the rain. We peddled so much food that guests were laughingly turning us away because they had eaten too much.

At one point, the sun broke through the clouds and everyone rushed back outdoors. Everything was wet and the ground was soggy, but we performed what outdoor games were permissible. By the end of the afternoon, we were exhausted. It felt as if we had set up three separate picnics that day.

We could have just canceled the event due to inclement weather, but we chose to work to make the most of the situation. It was not, by any means, an ideal situation for a picnic. Nothing seemed to go according to plan. It was certainly not the way 300 people had expected to spend their afternoon. Yet, it was a positive effort under difficult circumstances. The guests understood and appreciated our efforts. In all, everyone seemed to have a reasonably good afternoon.

We do not always have control over situations, but we do have control over our emotions and responses to those situations.

The Missing Clarinet

We were coordinating a large summertime dinner party for a client when we discovered that there had been a break down in communication. We had hired a three-piece combo, and a bass player showed up instead of the clarinet player which had been requested by the client. This might seem insignificant, but the combo was scheduled to perform both on the outdoor terrace for a cocktail reception and indoors during a formal dinner. Outdoors, they were to stroll among the guests, for there was no space to set up permanently. As you can imagine, strolling is tough on a bass player.

With 45 minutes until show time, something had to be done. We decided to secure a background music system which could play pre-recorded music. It was not the same as live, strolling musicians, but it was much better than no music at all. Our biggest challenge now was to beat the clock.

Just 30 seconds before the arrival of the first guest, we finished setting up a backup sound system for the outdoor reception. The combo played for dinner as planned.

It was, very simply, our mistake. No one knew it except for the client and us, and the client never complained. The guests had a delightful evening and never knew anything was askew. The rest of the evening went off without a hitch. Yet, because things were not quite right, we voluntarily refunded half of the money for the event and sent a letter of apology. We had not lived up to our own expectations, so we certainly could not expect our client to pay full price.

When you make a mistake, do your
best to correct or improve the
situation, then settle up fairly
with your customer.

A Customer is a Customer

Have you ever walked into a jewelry store wearing jeans and been passed over for the guy in the dark gray suit or the woman with rings on every finger? Perhaps you were there to purchase an engagement ring and they were just there for watch repairs. Even though you walked in the store first, the other customers seemed more important to the sales clerk.

Well, the opposite can happen too. I stopped by an electrical contractors' supply store one day on the way to a client meeting. I was wearing a suit and tie, and I was completely ignored by the sales staff. However, the guys driving the pick-up trucks and wearing coveralls received immediate attention. The sales staff assumed that I either was not very knowledgeable about electrical matters, was not going to make a significant purchase, or was lost. But how would they know without asking?

Just as we cannot judge a book by its cover, we cannot determine what customers needs are based on the way they dress. And even if we could, it is not professional to provide poor service or ignore customers just because they are different—be it the way they dress, their gender or their cultural background. You might be surprised who turns out to be among your best customers!

Treat customers equally—on a first come, first served basis.

INFORMATION PLEASE

It is very frustrating to me when companies raise their prices while lowering their standards of service. Our phone company is a perfect example.

When I call information, it is often because I need assistance, not just a number. Recently, a computer answered my call to information instead of an operator. Having a conversation with a computer is just about as impersonal as it gets.

The first thing the computer asks you is the city you are calling. Well, sometimes I just do not know. I might know that the business I need is somewhere near Atlanta, but I do not know if it is located in Alpharetta, Lawrenceville, Peachtree City or Snellville. The next thing the computer asks you is the listing. Haven't you ever needed someone's phone number, but all you know is their last name and perhaps a street address? The computer does not recognize this information.

If you are fortunate enough to know the city and exact listing, an operator then comes on briefly to say, "One moment please." The computer provides you with the number. Can you explain why the only thing a live operator would say is, "One moment please?" A computer asks questions and expects an answer. The operator just makes a statement. This seems backwards to me. If the operator comes on the line anyway, why couldn't this individual just handle the call? To add insult to injury, the phone company has doubled its fee for this service.

Fortunately, I have learned that you can simply press "O" to get an operator on the line. Of course, they do not tell you this when you call, so most people just hang up frustrated when they cannot get assistance. I have just started pressing "O" as soon as the computer answers to get the service I prefer for my fifty cents. Recently, I asked the operator why they changed the service. She responded that it saved them time and money. Upon further questioning, I learned that they receive frequent complaints about this new service. What is the point of operating an information service that makes it difficult to get information or upsets customers?

Do not forget the "customer" in "customer service."

Package to London

At one of the events we coordinated, our client received a large piece of artwork as a gift during a special presentation. Because of its size, our client, who lived in London, asked if we could ship it home for him, and we happily agreed.

Although the package was light—flat art packed in styrofoam—it was unusually large. We contacted the major delivery services for prices. Even though our package only weighed a few pounds, they each wanted up to $200 for the international delivery. I carried the package to our local post office, but they could not even accept a package this size.

I asked the clerk why their competitors in the private sector could handle a package this size but that the postal service could not. She did not know, but agreed that the regulation did not really make sense. She went to her supervisor for an answer. When she returned, she explained that the policy had to do with contracts and regulations with foreign governments. While the U.S. Postal Service was capable of handling a package that size, international contracts prohibited them from shipping it to certain countries.

Instead of just saying, "No," or pointing to the rule book, she responded to my questions by searching for an explanation. Her personal interest in my problem was greatly appreciated, even if it did not change the situation.

Two days later, when I was in the Post Office for another

purpose, the postal clerk asked if I had found a way to ship my package, once again showing interest in my needs.

Even when you have set rules to follow, you can acknowledge and attempt to respond to your customer's needs, leaving a positive impression.

BUTTERFINGERS

At one particular meeting, we used candy as part of our themed decorations. My client's representative visited the staging area often as we prepared for the meeting. During her visits, she would sample the assorted candies. It came to our attention that Butterfinger BBs® were her favorite selection.

Since we had more than enough candy for the event, we sent a case of the Butterfinger BBs® to her room. This simple gesture caught her attention, brought a smile to her face and created a lasting impression.

Several months later, we prepared similar decorations for another event. Purchasing candy brought to mind the smile on our client's face. Knowing how good it made both her and us feel, we decided, spur of the moment, to send her another case of Butterfinger BBs®. The attached note said, "Just thinking of you."

Simple gestures are almost always appreciated the most when they are least expected. Why not drop a note in the mail, make a call or send a small token of appreciation to your customers today...just to let them know that they are on your mind?

Remember your customers even when you are not working on a current job for them. Let them know that they are always remembered and appreciated.

TECHNICAL DIFFICULTIES

We were in charge of coordinating a special two day event for a client. We arranged everything from hotel rooms and transportation, to sound systems and entertainment, to catering and table decorations. Our business philosophy is to maintain a core staff to manage each event, while contracting with local services to provide additional support. Audiovisual services are among those for which we turn to local experts.

During the first day of the event, we noticed that there was a slight hum in the sound system. The technical support staff tested every connection, microphone, speaker and cable in the system. Finally, at the end of the day, they thought they had resolved the problem. The following morning, however, we noticed that there was still a slight hum in the system. Fortunately, the meeting could be conducted without distraction.

A few days later, while editing the videotape, we discovered that the hum was very noticeable on the recording. The keynote speaker had given a very personal, emotional speech at the event and my client wanted to have a videotape of this speech for future use. Unfortunately, the hum had distorted the sound on the video.

Although I had significant funds invested in this video production, I sent a copy to my client at no charge and with my sincerest apologies. Although the situation was out of my personal control, I was ultimately responsible for the production. It was important to acknowledge the mistake to my client and to resolve the issue.

There are times when we do not have complete control over a situation and it becomes more difficult to manage. Even so, we must do our best to make things right and to handle each situation professionally.

Handle your problems responsibly and professionally.

Free Breakfast—Service Not Included

Lake Havasu is a wonderful oasis in the desert. If you have never seen the London Bridge, a stop at Lake Havasu is a must.

During a vacation trip to Lake Havasu, our family stayed at a nice hotel near the London Bridge. Upon check-in, we were informed about a complimentary breakfast buffet.

The next morning when we arrived at the restaurant for our complimentary breakfast, we saw many empty tables, but had to wait to be seated because the tables had not been bussed. Once seated, we had to wait again. As we sat there hoping someone would be along soon to take our order, we noticed that the restaurant appeared chaotic. Nothing seemed to be organized or working efficiently

Finally, we placed our order. Renee and the children chose the buffet, while I selected something from the menu. Many items were missing from the buffet. My order was slow to arrive. Service was poor. It was obvious that the restaurant was understaffed and poorly managed.

When our check arrived, the total was incorrect. I asked politely to speak with the manager, but was informed that he was not available. However, the head chef did come out of the kitchen to speak with me. He had only recently been hired by the property managers. Even though he wasn't the manager, he listened intently to my concerns, apologized for the problems, and informed me that he was making every attempt to improve the entire operation. He further explained that the restaurant was in the midst of a management change, but agreed that this should be no excuse for the problems we encountered. He knew that he was fighting an uphill battle at this restaurant, but it was obvious that he was determined to make it work. This chef knew the recipe for success.

Listening is an important skill to master. By listening to your customers, you acknowledge that their opinions are important and can identify ways to improve customer service.

LITTLE THINGS ADD UP

When traveling through Virginia, we stayed at a hotel that was undergoing a major renovation. As a result of the renovation, we encountered several small annoyances.

For instance, in order to reach our rooms, we had to enter through the back door. When we needed to make a phone call, we discovered that the telephone did not work. The air conditioning unit made a terrible noise. And later, we found mold in the bathtub, wallpaper that was missing above the bathroom door and a dirty washcloth that had been left behind by housekeeping.

Individually, none of these items would have mattered much. Collectively, they made a real impression.

Finally, I decided to mention these items at the front desk. I was referred to the manager on duty. Though a young manager, he was genuinely concerned about my problems and wanted to make things right. He was very professional, apologized for the inconveniences, and agreed to do what he could to remedy the situation. Like the chef at the restaurant, he attributed the problems to changes, but quickly added that their renovations should not effect the service provided by the hotel.

All businesses go through changes of one kind or another as they grow. Keep your customers in mind when you undertake such changes. Customers should still receive the services that they are paying for.

Brown Sod

Not too long ago, we had new sod and an irrigation system installed in our yard. After obtaining bids from several landscape companies, we decided upon an independent contractor. This was a real investment for us, so we wanted to review contracts and pin down all of the details. When we asked what kind of deposit would be required, we were quite surprised when the contractor informed us that we did not have to pay until the job was done and we were satisfied. It was clear that he was confident in the quality of his work.

The landscape crew worked hard. They arrived on time each day. They cleaned up after digging. Everything they did was very neat and professional. The only problem we ran into involved several small patches of sod that were brown. When we pointed this out, the contractor simply wanted to fertilize the area and have me water it regularly for about 10 days. He thought it would turn green during that time. He even said I would not have to pay him until the grass turned green.

While this might be true, I was not satisfied with the solution. I felt the grass should be right when it was installed, not after I tended it for more than a week. It just didn't make sense that this contractor had been so professional about everything, but did not want to replace a few squares of sod to satisfy his customer. It was a little thing—a small detail that could have spoiled the otherwise positive service provided by the contractor. Finally, he recognized our dissatisfaction and honored our request by replacing the sod himself.

Let your customers know that you have confidence in your products and services. And remember to follow through on all the minor details, for they are often what the customer remembers most.

Part Four

EXCEPTIONAL SERVICE

When you exceed customer expectations, you leave a lasting impression. It is a strong lasting impression that can set you apart from your competition, thus making the biggest difference in your bottom line and long-term success.

GROUP PHOTOS

Any business runs into unexpected challenges or makes mistakes from time to time. The key to providing good customer service is how your business handles those situations, and whether or not you view them as problems or opportunities.

Things are anything but routine in our corporate entertainment business. Each event is different. Most of these events take place at off-site locations, so a lot of advance planning is required. Even so, we still face the unexpected from time to time.

For instance, we had planned to take a group photograph of a company's sales representatives during their three day meeting, which had an oldies theme. Rather than just line them up in rows, we brought in a beautiful 1957 pink and white Chevy Impala convertible for the photograph and arranged everyone casually around it. To ensure that the photograph had turned out, we had the film processed and delivered to the marketing director that afternoon.

He loved the photograph. In fact, he was so pleased that he asked if there was any way to get 145 enlargements printed, matted and shrink-wrapped by that evening for the sales representatives. The photographs could then be placed on the pillows in their rooms by the hotel staff prior to the closing of that night's events. We said we'd try.

During the next five hours, we found a photographer willing to make 145 11x14 prints and a frame shop to double mat and shrink wrap them. Then we worked with the hotel to arrange having them placed on the beds of all 145 sales representatives before the evening's activities were over. We pulled it off, but only because everyone—including our staff, the hotel, the photo lab and the frame shop—pitched in and worked together.

❧

Treat a challenge as a unique opportunity. Show your clients that you are willing to go that extra mile for them.

❧

And Then Came the Videos

After working all afternoon to pull together the 145 group photos, we stayed up all night to edit video footage that had been shot throughout the sales meeting. This required viewing and editing hours of footage for a four minute highlight video presentation. The presentation was scheduled for their closing session the next day.

At 7 a.m. the next morning, we showed the edited video to the marketing director for his final approval. Once again, he loved it. Since the sales representatives had been so pleased with their group photos, he wondered if there was any way to get 145 copies of the video before the closing session ended at noon. That way, each person could be handed a video before leaving to catch their planes. As before, we said we'd do everything we could to meet this deadline.

We started calling. And we started begging. Finally, we convinced our duplication company to accept the challenge. One of our employees who had already been up all night working on the production drove the master copy to the duplication facility. He slept in the car as copies were being made and boxed. With time to spare, he arrived back at the hotel with the copies. Thanks to everyone involved, we were able to meet our client's objectives.

Dealing with this unusual request, we not only won the confidence of this client, thus securing future contracts, but we were paid extra for the special services. So going that extra mile can pay off financially too.

Providing exceptional service is a great way to build loyalty among your customers or clients. Make it a policy to always attempt to meet special requests.

HELICOPTER FOR HIRE

At the end of this same three day sales meeting, I was conducting a wrap up session with the marketing director. He was very pleased with our efforts and said that he liked to work with people who would hire helicopters. Not having any idea what he meant, I asked him to explain. Here's the story he told me:

Transportation companies, such as overnight delivery services, rely heavily upon their communications systems. One transportation company was temporarily shut down when a major winter storm knocked out their communications tower. Because of the snow, no one could repair equipment at the tower. Business was at a stand still. Finally, an employee took the initiative to hire a helicopter to fly him to the tower, where he repaired the equipment.

"Now that's the kind of person I like to hire," said the marketing director. To this day, I'm always reminding myself and my employees about the importance of hiring helicopters. It's not just the ability to hire the helicopter, but the willingness to find a solution.

Providing exceptional service means doing what it takes to get the job done right, which sometimes requires a little ingenuity or going above and beyond what is expected or what is normal.

A Race with the Clock

Just as we were wrapping up a convention in Austin without a hitch, a small crisis hit. As everyone was sitting down for the closing banquet, the president of the host company remembered that he had forgotten to purchase a gift for the speaker. He had wanted to give a special international clock to the speaker, who traveled often and would appreciate its unique features. In a panic, the president turned to us for help. Could we find that clock, have it wrapped, and get it here by the end of the program—which was not much more than two hours away? We agreed to give it our best effort.

After making several quick calls, we found the clock—clear across town. We asked them if they could wrap and deliver the gift immediately. They agreed to the wrapping, but did not offer delivery services, so we sent one of our employees to pick up the gift. Since he had a walkie-talkie, we stayed in touch the entire time. Within the conference center, we used walkie-talkies to communicate as well. The minutes were counting down, we were all beginning to pace, and I'm sure our driver was exceeding the speed limit by more than he or I should care to admit.

Just as the speaker was wrapping up his remarks, our driver pulled up at the front of the hotel, tossed the wrapped gift out the window to our field supervisor, who ran at top speed down the hotel corridors and behind the conference room stage—just in time to hand the gift to the president as he took the stage to thank the keynote speaker.

Everyone's adrenaline was pumping. We had beat the clock by mere moments. More importantly, we had come to the rescue of our client and met his needs.

Learn to recognize potential problems as opportunities to provide exceptional service.

BOTTLED WATER

S pecial events are our business. We often look for ways to
provide a personal touch—to do the unexpected. For one
event, we discovered at the last minute that the president of
the company and another important attendee preferred drink-
ing LeCroix water in a bottle. The meeting was to be held in
Texas, and LeCroix water was only available in cans in that
state.

Upon calling the home office of LeCroix, we determined
that our best bet was to have the bottled water shipped from
Georgia. It was late Friday afternoon, but the owner of Dixie
Distributors was happy to help us out by shipping the water to
us on Saturday for Sunday delivery.

Unfortunately, the delivery company handling the ship-
ment did not deliver the water as scheduled and could not
track down our package within their system. With only one
day left before our meeting, we called the owner of Dixie
Distributors at home. It was a Sunday afternoon and we knew
his business would be closed. His wife answered, was sympathetic to our needs, and kindly took an order for twelve cases
of LeCroix bottled water. Later that afternoon, her husband
went down to the warehouse and pulled the cases of bottled
water. We made arrangements with an overnight delivery service for pick up, and the water arrived in Texas the next morning just in time for the meeting.

We had never done business before with Dixie Distributors, and the owner had no reason to believe that we ever would again. Yet, he went out of his way to help us, because that's just the way he runs his business. Knowing I might not have an opportunity to make future purchases from him, I sent a note and gift to show our appreciation.

Providing exceptional service is a way of doing business that doesn't always require a lot of thought or contemplation. Action is a natural response to a customer in need.

CORNED BEEF AND CABBAGE

Coming from an Irish family, St. Patrick's Day is a special occasion. One St. Patrick's Day, as we were proudly wearing our green, we stopped at a hotel restaurant for dinner on the way to the hospital to visit my mom. The restaurant had an Irish buffet with a great selection of entrees, including corned beef and cabbage.

On our way out, we asked the manager if we could purchase a "to go" plate for my dad, who was spending his days at the hospital with mom. My father is as Irish as they come. Since corned beef and cabbage ranks among his favorite meals, I thought this might brighten his day.

A few minutes later, the manager came out with a large plate of corned beef and cabbage and a smile. When I asked what we owed, he said, "Nothing. I hope your father enjoys it."

This was completely unexpected, and I could tell that it made the manager feel good. He was proud of his food and service. He was pleased that we wanted to share his food with someone in order to brighten their day. He was a generous business man who knew the value of pleasing customers.

St. Patrick's Day was just the first of many visits to this restaurant. We are regulars now, and we refer our friends there often. A single plate of food from an Irish buffet cost him little. But it brightened my dad's day—his Irish eyes were smiling— secured our loyalty, and generated new business from our referrals. That is the kind of loyalty that you cannot buy with advertising.

Surprise someone. Do the unexpected. Discover the true value of providing exceptional service…it is far greater than advertising.

To Plug or Patch?

The dealership where I purchased my car is several hours away from where I live, so I do my best to avoid needing any special servicing. However, the manufacturer had issued a recall notice and my car had been making an annoying squeaking noise, so I called the local dealer to make an appointment.

They needed two days to complete the repairs. When I dropped the car off, the clerk at the service desk wanted to provide me with a loaner car of equal stature, but there were not any available. Just as we were emptying the trunk of my car, in drove a car similar to my own. The only problem was, it had a flat tire. The clerk said he would like for me to take that car, provided I did not mind waiting while they repaired the tire.

As they repaired the tire, I walked back to their garage area and loaded my things into the trunk. While I was there, the mechanic found a screwdriver in the flat tire. For safety reasons, he decided to patch the tire instead of plug it, so he headed off to the storage room for supplies. As I waited, I could not help but notice how busy this place was. There were at least 20 cars in the shop, all of them receiving the serious attention of mechanics.

About that time, the service desk clerk noticed that I was still waiting. With a concerned look on his face, he came and spoke with the mechanic. I could not hear what they were saying, but I got the distinct impression that they were discussing my situation and the reason for my wait.

The mechanic came over and said that they were out of patches and that the nearest auto supply store was 20 minutes away. With that news, I suggested just plugging the hole since I wasn't traveling far. Concerned about a blowout and my safety, the mechanic disagreed. While we discussed the alternatives, the clerk from the service desk drove up in the other loaner car. I figured he was going to hand me the keys. Instead, he handed the mechanic a tire patch. When he realized what the problem was, he took the other loaner car, drove to the service station next door and purchased a patch. Just four minutes later, I was on my way.

This was a clerk who kept an eye on his customers. He thought on his feet and came up with a solution that was much quicker than normal procedures. And in a very low key way, he took the initiative to resolve the problem. He did what it took to satisfy the customer.

Taking care of customers often means keeping an eye on things—even after you have completed your own duties.

WILL YOU TAKE MY CHECK?

I often cringe when I think of writing a check when I'm on the road. Out-of-state checks are rarely accepted, and when they are, it seems you need to have your life history in your wallet. It is a wonder the hoops we sometimes jump through just to make a purchase.

We were in West Palm Beach for a company sales meeting in which there were non-stop activities and events—ranging from banquets and receptions, to scuba diving and tennis, to beach volleyball and pool parties. We needed refreshments, and lots of them. In fact, we needed 26 cases of beer, 27 cases of soft drinks and 10 cases of bottled water.

My wife, Renee—armed with a company check, my personal credit card and her own out-of-state driver's license—set out to purchase some beverages. And she was prepared for the headache of getting a check approved.

She knew a local food warehouse would have what she needed, so she called one of them to see if they would accept her check. The young lady who answered the phone transferred her call to Steve. Renee explained her situation, what she needed, how she'd like to pay, and what identification she had available. Steve said the check would be fine, and that he would have everything ready for her when she arrived. Pleasantly surprised, Renee gave him a detailed breakdown by brand, thanked him, and drove over in the car.

Upon her arrival, Steve greeted her and said the order was

ready. There was just one problem. One of the brands of beer ordered was only available in a bottle, and we needed cans. But he had located the canned beer at a nearby store and they had already pulled several cases for us. Finally, he opened a vacant register, rang up our order and accepted our out-of-state check (checking our available identification). Then he carried the drink cases to our car on a dolly and helped us load everything up. The car was packed to the limit.

It is nice to know that some companies—even a discount warehouse—will still go out of their way to make doing business with them a pleasure.

One of the secrets to success is making it easy for people to do business with your company.

THE CADDIE

I love golf. I have always enjoyed the sport and play whenever the opportunity arises. Recently, I had a chance to play a round at Pinehurst #2 in North Carolina. There are 18 courses at Pinehurst. Pinehurst #2 is their most famous course. The U.S. Open has been hosted here and the place is steeped in tradition.

On this occasion, I even had a caddie for the round. He did all the things a caddie is supposed to do. He carried my bag, wiped my balls clean, helped me judge the distance to the green, and let me know which way my ball would break as it rolled toward the hole. He went beyond the call of duty as well. For instance, he loaned me a personal towel when we were starting out because he knew the temperature would reach near 95 degrees that day. He wiped my clubs dry after each shot. He told me the history of the course and shared his personal experiences with notable golfers. He had such kind words for the course and all the golfers he had met. He was relaxed, thoughtful, and very attentive to details. He was a perfect gentleman—very subtle, with kind words and conversation. As a caddie, he was the epitome of service.

At the end of the afternoon, when he was loading my bag into the car, I asked him about his work. He was in the landscape business. For the past 33 years, he had cut grass in the morning and caddied in the afternoon. He was a happy man, doing what he liked. Because he enjoyed his work so much, he

124

was very good at being a caddie, and probably at landscaping tasks as well. Although I wasn't too pleased with my score on the course, I had a delightful day thanks to my caddie.

When we enjoy and are dedicated to our work, customers notice the difference. A positive attitude is contagious.

Shop at Home

I have never cared much about shopping for clothes. While I like to feel comfortable and look good in the clothes I wear, I am just not what you would call a "clothes hound." In fact, I like having someone to help me coordinate suits and ties when I shop, and to give advice on the styles I should wear. Unfortunately, now that independent clothiers are competing with national retail chains, it is getting more and more difficult to find that level of personalized service.

I come from a small town in Georgia where there is a men's and ladies' specialty clothing shop that still does business "the old fashioned way." Despite the increased competition, they've continued to offer first class service. It is how they built their business and their customers appreciate the extra effort.

At this store, there is a salesperson named Connie who has made clothes shopping not only bearable, but a pleasant experience for me. She knows my sizes and the type of clothes I prefer, so she calls when something new arrives that she thinks I would like. If I am interested, she drops the clothing off by the house—allowing me to try them on at my convenience— then picks them back up a few days later. I can do all of my shopping without even going in the store.

She does this for many of her customers. She understands that it is difficult to get to the store and works hard to satisfy the needs of her customers on their schedule. In fact, I understand that Connie has never even met one of her customers—a woman who lives in another town, several hours away. One day, this woman called and said she was familiar with the store. Would they ship some clothes for her to try? After asking some questions about sizes, favorite colors and preferred styles, Connie shipped her several selections on an approval basis, and she continues to do so frequently.

The other thing I really like about doing business with this store is that I can call and tell them I need a gift. They will select something appropriate, based on my guidelines, then wrap and deliver it. Their entire sales staff provides this level of service, and they do it for a salary, not a commission. Over the years, they have built their business and their individual careers on providing exceptional service.

∞

To provide exceptional service, identify customer needs and go above the expected level of service to meet those needs.

∞

HOTEL MENUS

In West Palm Beach, we have found a first class hotel that our clients just love. They have consistently provided some of the best service we have ever encountered in a hotel or convention center. I can always count on them to come through with any job. I have never heard them say "No" or "We cannot do that."

I had been bragging to one of my clients about the great service we always received at this hotel. Since they were looking for a site for a sales meeting, they decided that they would like to take a look around this hotel. Without alerting the hotel of our plans, we met in West Palm Beach and I gave my client a tour of their facilities while we discussed the possibilities for their meeting.

When we walked into the restaurant, my client asked me about the menus and food service. There was only one other person in the restaurant at the time—a restaurant employee who was doing final touch up before dinner. My client asked her if she might see a menu. The employee responded by handing my client a leather bound lunch menu. As we were looking it over, she asked if we might also need menus for other meals, then immediately returned with the lunch and dinner menus, which she informed us we could keep.

This was a wonderful example of proper training and attention to details. She knew the importance of assisting customers—even when it went beyond the normal duties detailed in her job description. Hotel management had instilled enough confidence in her to respond to our request instead of just referring us to a manager or the catering department. Someone had taught her the importance of never saying "no" to a customer. My client and I were both surprised and impressed.

Employee training should include more than policies and procedures. It should emphasize the role every employee has in serving customers.

FOSSILS AND GEMSTONES

For her history class, my daughter had to identify Georgia's state fossil, gemstone and wildflower. What sounded like an easy assignment turned out to be a real research project. She checked the encyclopedia, looked it up through our on-line computer service, called several friends and asked another teacher or two. The information eluded her.

The next day, it occurred to me that the Secretary of State's office would probably have this information. I called, but the line was consistently busy. Since their number ended in four different digits, I tried dialing the same number with "00" as the last two digits, thinking this might reach a general information number. Instead, it connected me with the State Superintendent's office. I explained to the secretary that I was trying to identify the state's fossil, gemstone and wildflower, but could not get through to the Secretary of State's office. She said to hold while she transferred my call to someone who might help. I got a recording, but she immediately came back on the line. She tried several other numbers, each time getting a recording or busy signal. Laughing, she said, "Don't you just hate that!"

After apologizing for the inability to get through to anyone, she said that if I had time to wait, she'd see if there was any information in her computer. She had never tried looking up this type of information, but was willing to give it a try.

Just a moment later, she squealed with joy. "I found it!"

she said, quite surprised. "The state fossil is the shark's tooth. There is a long list of all the official state designations, as well as another list that gives a brief history explaining why each one was chosen. If you like, I will be happy to fax you both lists."

A few minutes later, I received the fax. This wasn't her usual job. She was just providing good service and helping out wherever she could. In helping us research this information, she also assisted with my daughter's education and learned a bit more about her own computer capabilities. Grateful for her assistance, my daughter sent her a thank you note.

Sometimes, when we go that extra mile, we surprise even ourselves or learn new things to assist us in our own work.

CHEESECAKE

For vacation this year, we drove up the east coast, stopping at many historic sites. Two of our children are in elementary school, at just about the right ages to enjoy the Smithsonian Institute, Williamsburg and other important places.

On July 5, we were passing through Binghamton, New York and stopped by a sports bar for lunch. It was a slow day after an unusually busy Independence Day, and the restaurant was out of many items. However, the waitress spent plenty of time with us, was very gracious, and said that the chef would do his very best to fix whatever we wanted.

Although they were out of many of the menu items we requested, the chef prepared a nice meal for us. When we requested cheesecake for dessert, there was a slight pause before our waitress said, "Sure, I'll be back with that in just a moment."

When she finally arrived with the cheesecake, she said, "I'm sorry this took so long. I had to run down the street for it."

Just a few doors down from the restaurant is a coffee shop that serves desserts. The restaurant was out of cheesecake, but rather than tell us this, she went to the coffee shop to buy a slice. I guess she just could not bear to tell us that they were out of anything else. Since it was a slow day, she could slip away to get it.

Thanks to the splendid service she provided under difficult circumstances, she earned a generous tip and we will definitely stop there again if we are ever in Binghamton.

Approach a difficult situation as a challenge. Be creative and take pride in finding new ways to serve your customers.

HUMAN NATURE

On this same vacation, but in a different restaurant, I left the table to take our two year old to the rest room. When I returned, the waiter and manager were tending my wife, Renee, with orange juice, water and ice packs.

Without warning, Renee had become sick and felt very faint. The restaurant staff responded immediately, showing real concern and compassion. When I arrived, they gave me directions to the nearest emergency room, boxed up all of our food to go, and helped us get the kids to the car.

Although we spent several hours in the emergency room, Renee is fine. We both appreciated the concern and assistance of the restaurant staff. They not only were prepared for an emergency, they let us see their "human side." They were just as helpful as could be.

Prepare in advance for possible emergencies. Whether you have an emergency or not, let your customers know that you are human and care about their well being.

ROOM SERVICE

It was the night the Braves won the World Series. We had been in charge of a client event that evening and returned to our Atlanta hotel room very late. Exhausted and hungry, we called room service. They were closed.

However, the front desk clerk knew we had just come in from work and asked what we wanted. We told her and she said, "I'll see what I can do."

About ten minutes later, there was a knock on our door. It was the front desk clerk. She had found the key to the kitchen and scrounged around for some milk, coffee, cookies and other snacks for us to eat. Although she couldn't prepare any meals, she had found a few things to hold us over until breakfast. When we offered her a tip, she refused. She just wanted to help out where she could.

Showing that you care and understand is the way to the hearts of your customers.

THE MASK

For those with children, Halloween is always filled with surprises. This past year, our three-year-old son wanted to be a Power Ranger®. Evidently, so did every other child. There are a lot of costume shops in Atlanta, but it seemed that they had all sold out of this popular costume.

Finally, we found just what we were looking for at Holiday Costume Company and headed home. Only, when we took the costume out of the bag, there was no mask. This may sound insignificant, but we suddenly had a distraught three-year-old on our hands and something had to be done immediately. Halloween was just 24 hours away.

We called the costume store and explained our predicament. They apologized and offered to send us a mask by overnight delivery. Since our daughter had just decided to be a witch for this special occasion, we asked if they might include a black hat and cape in the package—adding this to our bill.

Everything arrived the next morning by overnight delivery, yet they did not charge us for a thing. Instead, they recognized that we had been inconvenienced by the missing mask and went a step beyond what was expected to make sure that we were satisfied with our costumes and could enjoy the holiday. I know where we'll shop first for our Halloween costumes in the future.

✎

Learn to recognize opportunities
to do more than is expected for
your customers. It is a great way
to build loyalty.

✎

INFLATABLES

One of the parties we planned for a corporate event had a 1960s theme. As employees and guests entered the ballroom, "Magic Carpet Ride" would fill the room with sound, an inflatable saxophone or guitar would be placed in every seat, and everyone would be given a pair of John Lennon style glasses to wear. On the tables were small, spinning laser discs that light up in a thousand different colors. In other words, we were filling the room with energy and fun.

Putting together a major theme party is a big job, so we do as much as possible in advance. One of our pre-event activities was blowing up the inflatable musical instruments— 2,000 of them. We did this three weeks prior to the event, then placed them in bags and onto a truck for cross-country shipping.

We arrived in Denver for our event two days ahead of time to finalize all arrangements and to begin setting up. When we got to the inflatables, they were anything but inflated. All 2,000 guitars and saxophones had holes in them. As it turns out, we had not taken into account that the truck would have to go over mountains to arrive in Denver, where the air is much thinner. This caused the inflatables to expand and pop.

The inflatables were central to our decorations and carrying out our theme. We simply had to have them. We checked our warehouse in Atlanta, but did not have enough in stock. So, our event coordinator called Oriental Trading in Omaha,

Nebraska—our original source for the inflatables. He explained the situation to a supervisor and asked if there was any way to get a new order on a plane that day.

Although we are a regular customer of this company, we are not an especially large one. Furthermore, this was our problem, not theirs. The supervisor wasn't familiar with our account, but said he would take care of it. That day, he pulled the stock, drove it to the airport himself, and saw that it was loaded onto the plane. In Denver, our event coordinator waited on their arrival and then drove them to the hotel. Our staff stayed up all night blowing up these 2,000 inflatables. By 7 a.m., our saxophones and guitars were in place, ready for the opening session. The client never knew we skipped a beat. The supervisor in Omaha had saved the day.

By helping customers solve problems, you develop a long-lasting and loyal customer base.

Part Five

CUSTOMER SERVICE IS A TWO WAY STREET

Much of customer service is based on customer expectations, so we should expect only the best. If we expect less, less is exactly what we will receive.

Can You Help Me?

In my business, we get a lot of unusual requests. Clients love something new…something different… something memorable. For one corporate client, we were planning special races at a company gathering. Their advertising slogan incorporated a racing theme, so they suggested go-carts.

We wanted to rent go-carts due to the cost of purchasing them, but we knew that finding go-cart rentals would be difficult. Our first call was to a family entertainment complex that offered go-cart racing, miniature golf, pinball machines and other activities. Knowing in advance that they probably would not rent to us, I started my phone conversation with, "Can you help me?"

There is just something about human nature. We love to feel needed. We like to lend a helping hand.

The person who answered the phone was very helpful. She said that they did not rent go-carts due to liability issues, but gave me the name of several companies that sold go-carts. There was absolutely nothing in this for her. I wasn't going to spend any money with her company. Yet, I was polite and allowed her to assist me. As a result, I received some information that was helpful in my search.

This strategy of asking for assistance—instead of just telling someone what I need—works almost every time. Those four simple words, "Can you help me?" are among the strongest tools we have in our business.

It also pays to turn those words around. For instance, whenever we talk with clients or potential customers, we ask, "How can we help you?"

Immediately, they know we are interested in their needs. I have seen this work especially well when dealing with difficult customers. Showing kindness, sincerity and genuine concern is the fastest way to cool off a hot customer.

A secret to giving and receiving good customer service is understanding that people like to help and be helped.

THE BAD ATTITUDE BRIDE

O ccasionally, since we are in the entertainment and events business, we handle wedding receptions. One reception stands out among all the rest.

It was a beautiful event. The flowers were gorgeous; the food was delicious; the band gave a flawless performance; guests were in a festive mood. The hotel, caterer and florist had all done an outstanding job. The bride, groom and parents all seemed pleased with the results.

After the honeymoon, we received a call from the bride. She was not happy with the job we had done. The reception, she said, was not at all what she had planned. She demanded a refund, and that is what we gave her for our portion of the services. Next we heard from the caterer, the florist and the hotel. She had demanded refunds from them as well. We were all dumbfounded.

After making a few calls, we discovered that this woman had treated other local vendors in the same fashion. She contracted for services, then later complained and demanded a refund. I may never understand why, but apparently she considers it a game to see how much she can get for free. That is the wrong attitude to have, and one day it will backfire on her. This reputation will spread and no one will be willing to work with her at all.

If you have a problem with the service that has been provided to you, by all means let your concerns be known. And when you do, make it your goal to resolve the problem—not just to receive something for free. Never file a complaint without justifiable cause.

While you shouldn't have to pay for poor service, the purpose of filing a complaint is to resolve a problem, not to get something for free.

Ballroom Dancing

Growing up in a small southern community, my mother and the other mothers in our town sent their children to ballroom dancing classes. We were all at the age when ballroom dancing seemed a little goofy, but even the guys had fun because they got to dance with the girls, and at least everyone was doing this sort of silly stuff together. In fact, it made for great conversation at school the next day.

What we did not realize at the time was that it was not so much the dancing, but the etiquette, that our parents hoped we would learn in our ballroom dancing classes. They knew it was important for us to learn proper manners, and that sometimes it was more effective to learn it in a fun way.

Customer service should be taught in a similar fashion—not in ballroom dancing classes, but in a fun way when our children are young. When we take our children to a restaurant, to the grocery store, to a clothing shop or to some other business, we should take time to point out examples of both good and not-so-good customer service. We can even make a fun game out of this. A brief discussion in the car on the way home can give our children a chance to talk about why they were impressed or unimpressed with the way they were served, and how poor service might have been improved. It always amazes me how aware children are of such details.

By occasionally discussing the service that we receive from others, we can build a foundation of understanding and a good attitude about customer service in our children. This attitude will help our children succeed in the business world that they will undoubtedly enter one day.

Like good manners, it is important to learn about customer service at a young age.

Noisy Toilets

There are seven toilets in our house. Count them...seven. When we moved in, five of the seven were broken. Some would run all day. Others would begin running mysteriously in the middle of the night. The sound itself was very annoying and I hated thinking of the water we were wasting.

A local plumber made many trips to work on the problem. He would manage to fix most of them, but after awhile, they always began running again. After several visits, he suggested that we replace the toilets. Although it was expensive, we replaced two of the toilets. We purchased the same brand so that all of our toilets would match. Before long, these toilets were having problems too, and it became clear that our plumber had given up.

In desperation, we called the manufacturer, hoping to speak with someone in customer service. We weren't sure where the company was located, but as it turned out, it was very early in that time zone and the president answered the telephone. He listened to Renee's story and said he was amazed at how much she knew about toilets. In fact, since she knew more about their operation than he did, he said he would have an engineer call her back later that morning. The engineer called within an hour.

He was very helpful and agreed to send her some parts for free. As it turned out, all we needed was a few washers.

Three weeks later, the president called back. He wanted to

thank us for contacting him. This was his company, and it was not often that he received calls from users of his products. We had provided him with some useful information, and he wanted to make sure that our problem had been resolved.

Remember that company owners and managers usually do want to know what is on your mind. You may be surprised by how receptive and helpful they can be. And remember, they are the ones who make business decisions.

A POOR PRESENTATION

One of our clients had an important employee presentation to make. It would require a special projector that would communicate with their computer, so I arranged for an audiovisual company to provide the specialized equipment. I also coordinated a meeting of all parties involved.

The next day, I arrived on location for the meeting, but the audiovisual company did not. When I called, they apologized for the breakdown in communication and said they would be on their way immediately.

Finally, a representative arrived, we had our meeting, and arrangements were made for the client presentation. However, we were informed that a different representative would be sent to handle the on-site job.

I told them, "Absolutely not. Continuity is important. We need someone on-site who has discussed this project with the client."

They already dropped the ball by forgetting today's meeting. Sending someone unfamiliar with my client and his specific needs to handle an important job was simply not acceptable.

Finally, they agreed and we finalized all the details.

The program was to begin at 6:00 a.m. the following morning, but the audiovisual technicians arrived 30 minutes late.

To make matters worse, there were several glitches in the program because the sound technician was not paying attention to details.

I was unable to be present for this job, but quickly got word of the problems, and later tried to help them work out the bugs. However, the second day of the meeting, the technicians were late again and problems persisted.

By this time, my client was beginning to get annoyed, and with good cause. He let me know that if we could successfully handle large and complex events, this little presentation should be a snap. He was absolutely right.

I contacted the manager at the audiovisual company immediately and explained my problems.

Not long afterwards, the president of the company called me directly and wanted to know all of the details. He was very apologetic, said that this definitely was not acceptable, and was not the way they had trained employees to conduct business.

In short, he was embarrassed by the situation, but very appreciative that I had alerted him to the problem. He made a personal commitment to resolve the problem immediately, said that he hoped I would not judge his company based on this one incident, and gave me his direct phone number to call whenever I had a need in the future.

I have used this company many times through the years. With this one exception, their service has always been outstanding. If I had not called, similar problems might also have been experienced by other clients—so they appreciated being informed.

Do not judge a person or company based on a single experience. Let them know if there is a problem, then give them another chance if they resolve that problem and show genuine concern.

Part Six

THE BOTTOM LINE IN CUSTOMER SERVICE

The bottom line is that people provide customer service. By providing good customer service, you can make a difference in your company's bottom line.

Making Money by Meeting Customer Needs

The ability to provide quality service is directly related to our ability to succeed financially. If you can provide good customer service, you can make money. If you can provide exceptional service on a consistent basis, you can usually charge more for your products and services.

The impact of customer service on the bottom line is direct. Just ask anyone who works on a commission basis or for tips. The salespersons who demonstrate that they can best meet their customer's needs get the job, assignment or sale. Those who are not as sensitive to their customer's needs do not. In a restaurant or any business in which employees earn tips, it is those individuals who have the best attitude and take care of their customers that command the most generous tips.

Even though it may not be as obvious, the same applies to businesses of all sizes. If your business can meet customer needs by providing the product or service desired in a pleasant and helpful manner, it will generate business. Even if you have the right product, you will lose business if the service doesn't meet customer expectations.

Improving customer service doesn't have to cost you a penny. While many large corporations spend thousands of dollars to implement quality service programs, all it really takes is the right attitude. Consider the following ways to improve customer service and your bottom line without spending a small fortune:

- Lead by example, for a customer service attitude starts at the top. Show your employees that you are committed to meeting customer needs and that you expect them to do the same.

- During staff meetings, brainstorm with employees about ways to improve customer service.

- Talk about the importance of customer service—giving specific examples—during your current training programs for company policies and procedures.

- Take time to evaluate your company policies and procedures. Do they prevent employees from providing good customer service? If so, modify them.

- Emphasize to employees that certain procedures can sometimes be bypassed in order to better serve customers.

- Recognize your employees when they exceed customer expectations or take special initiatives to meet customer needs. It can be as simple as telling them they did the right thing, presenting them with a certificate of recognition, or giving them a special reward—such as movie tickets or dinner for two.

- Ask your customers for their opinion. You can do this by circulating among and talking with customers or by providing survey cards for them to respond in private.

- Make sure that your employees understand that what is right is much more important than who is right.

We have built our company based on referrals and repeat

business. You can do the same. We all know that it costs a lot more to acquire new customers than it does to keep existing ones. You can reduce your marketing budget, or at least shift funds into new programs, by serving your existing customers well. Not only will they return, but they will tell their friends and business associates about you.

In our business, we have never spent money on media advertising. We have never needed to. That is because we know that actions speak much louder than words. Remember, one generous deed is worth far more than any advertising you could buy, and costs much less. Serve your customers well and they will do your marketing for you.

25 Principles of Customer Service

- Service is not everything. The desire and willingness to provide service is what is most important.

- Excellence in service can be seen anywhere. Although the level of services provided may vary from one business to another, a customer service attitude should always prevail.

- Customer service is based on meeting or exceeding customer expectations. Always strive to exceed customer expectations.

- A customer service attitude starts at the top. Business owners and managers must lead by example.

- When setting guidelines for customer service, keep it simple—encouraging employees to just "do what is right" for customers.

- Good customer service comes from the heart. It is honest, sincere, courteous, helpful and caring.

- Always say "thank you." Let your customers know that you appreciate their business.

- We all make mistakes from time to time. It is how we handle those mistakes that makes the biggest difference in the long run.

- Look for chances to provide exceptional service. Approach problems as opportunities.

- While individual efforts are important, providing customer service requires team work.

- Turn the tables on a situation. Take a look at the other side by putting yourself in your customers' shoes.

- Be aware of successes and failures around you. Learning from them will help you achieve success.

- Provide your services confidently. If you make a mistake: acknowledge it, correct the situation and move on.

- Do what it takes to get the job done while providing good service.

- Providing simple service can keep you in business. Providing exceptional service can set you apart from your competition and boost your bottom line.

- Customers should never have to work harder at buying something than you work at selling it.

- In our fast paced society, remember that time is money. Do not waste your customers' time.

- Remember, it is not your employer, but customers who ultimately provide your paycheck.

- A positive attitude is contagious, even among negative customers.

- Providing good service one day is a start. To excel in customer service requires an ongoing commitment.

- Providing good customer service takes practice. In time, it will come naturally.

- Most procedures should be viewed as guidelines. Common sense and necessity should guide decision-making.

- Always remember the power of a smile.

- The principles of good service are best learned at an early age, but it is never too late to start.

- Appreciate and communicate with your customers at all times, not just when you are seeking additional business.

Ten Tips for Getting the Service You Deserve

- Expect good service. When we accept poor service, we lower the standards for customer service. In time, those lower standards will become the norm.

- Keep a positive attitude. Search for a solution, not just an outlet for your frustration.

- Ask for assistance and use the word "help." It is human nature to want to help someone who needs assistance. People generally respond positively when someone asks for help.

- Remember that everyone makes a mistake now and then. Do not judge them based on the mistake itself, but on how they handle correcting the mistake.

- If you have a problem, find someone who cares, understands and will listen to your concerns. Sometimes this means approaching the manager or owner.

- Document everything, if possible. Managers usually need times, dates, names, locations and other specifics in order to resolve a specific problem.

- Most managers want to know if there is a problem. Keep in mind that you may be helping them, as well as the next customer, by pointing out errors or inefficiencies.

- Show confidence—not timidness or anger—when you file a complaint. This will earn greater respect and a more positive response.

- Do not judge a business based on a single incident, unless that incident cannot be resolved. Instead, judge a business based on a pattern of failures. It is better to evaluate a business on its overall track record, because everyone makes mistakes from time to time.

- Give a business and its employees a chance to make things right.

ORDER INFORMATION

Order *How Do You Spell Customer Service? CA$H* from
Event Management Solutions by Entertainment Ltd.
Toll Free at 1-800-338-5142 or send $14.95 plus
$2.50 for shipping and handling. Add $.50 for each
additional book. Quantity discounts are available.
Please contact **Event Management Solutions**
at 1-800-338-5142.

Mike McGraw is available for Keynote Presentations.
For more information, contact Mike at
Event Management Solutions toll free at
1-800-338-5142.

Please send _____ book(s).

Name: _____

Address: _____

_____

City: _____

State: _____ Zip: _____

Telephone: _____

Send check or money order (payable to *Event
Management Solutions*) plus above information to:

**Event Management Solutions by
Entertainment Ltd.
83 Clark Street
Newnan, GA 30263
(800) 338-5142**